40 Dives, 40 Dishes

Dive Stories and Recipes
from the
MV Salutay

by

Al and Freda Wright

Sandsmedia Publishing
BALI, INDONESIA

Editing and formatting by Simon Pridmore and Sofie Hostyn

Food styling by Freda Wright

Sandsmedia Publishing, Bali, Indonesia 80363

Book Layout ©2018 Createspace.com and Sandsmedia

Cover Images: Sherman tank by Steve Jones, other images by Freda Wright

40 Dives, 40 Dishes: Dive Stories and Recipes from MV Salutay 1st ed.

ISBN-13: 978-1717270788

ISBN-10: 1717270786

Table of Contents

Testimonials

"Salutay under the leadership of Alan and Freda Wright is the best UK liveaboard dive boat I have ever been aboard. The superb skippering and diving skills of Al Wright are only matched by Freda's culinary skills in the galley, producing haute cuisine. Always a pleasure to spend time on board and I will be back." **Jack Ingle: BSAC National Instructor**

"I have dived with Salutay for many years. This book brings together two amazing aspects of diving with them: not only spectacular dives, but wonderful food as well. Both Al and Freda work hard to create memorable dive trips and the combination of some of the best diving in the world and Freda's great food make this book a very welcome read." **Jane Maddocks MA: BSAC National Instructor and Underwater Cultural Heritage Advisor**

"In the late 90s, word of mouth coming out of Northern Ireland was that the wrecks were very good, the MV Salutay was the boat to dive off and Freda's cooking was to be savoured. While I have still not managed to dive the Northern Irish wrecks, after 21 years of wanting and waiting, I did get to dive off the Salutay and taste Freda's cooking. Do you know what? The rumours were well founded. It was all well worth the wait! Now with the release of this cookery book, you can get to enjoy a taste of the MV Salutay experience in your own home." **Rosemary E. Lunn (Roz): Underwater Marketing Company**

"MV Salutay offers that irresistible combination of stunning UK dives, skipper expertise, and blissful food. It's a 'must do' UK diving experience. Freda and Al Wright are a dream team: both are accomplished divers and excellent hosts. They inspire confidence, and that means people can relax and enjoy themselves. And I've witnessed Freda's roast dinners actually working miracles: bringing harmony and melting the hearts of even the grumpiest of British divers!" **Louise Trewavas: Extreme Ironing Scuba Depth World Record Holder**

"The Salutay is known for its adventures in Irish and Scottish waters, the English Channel and Normandy, renowned as a pioneering British technical diving liveaboard and famous for its restaurant-quality food. Al's knowledge of wrecks and all things technical and his dry Irish sense of humour make the diving side easy. Freda's food is amazing, not the usual British liveaboard menu. it is so special that it makes you feel that you are really on a holiday not just a dive trip. How she can cook like that on a boat and for a large number of hungry divers, I'll never know. **Sally Cartwright: Ex Chairman Sub-Aqua Association**

"The names MV Salutay and Al Wright are synonymous with the iconic Malin Head wrecks. MV Salutay was the very first boat that allowed technical divers to dive and explore these sites in the early 1990s. The pioneering work of the crews of MV Salutay has been a major influence on wreck diving of the North Coast of Ireland." **Barry McGill: Deep Wreck Photographer & Technical Diving Instructor (Indepth Technical Diving)**

The Authors

Al Wright is a RYA Yacht Master Offshore Commercial skipper with 30-years' experience operating commercial craft. A passionate technical diver who trained with and worked for Billy Deans, at Key West Divers, Florida in the early '90s, Al was one of the first trimix divers in the UK. Operating the MV Salutay to Rathlin Island and Malin Head, he discovered - and was the first to dive - the big three wrecks off Malin Head: HMS Audacious, RMS Justicia, and the SS Empire Heritage. A lead diver on Kevin Gurr's 1997 HMHS Britannic expedition and DIR rebreather 2017 expedition. Al is an IANTD trimix instructor on multiple units. Between operating charters on the MV Salutay, he is also a test diver for VMS, testing the Sentinel Redhead rebreather, and for Avon Protection.

Freda Wright is an accomplished IANTD trimix and cave diver and a trained chef. Her passion is cooking, particularly making cakes. As well as being responsible for all the catering on board the MV Salutay, Freda is in charge of bookings, so she's the first one you talk to when you make a reservation. She also dives on trips as much as she can and knows the dive sites the Salutay visits very well. When not under the water, Freda will often be found on top of the water on her paddleboard, as she is a keen and BCU 3- star qualified sea paddler.

30 Years At Sea: Diving Highlights

1. The Salutay Story

The MV Salutay was built in 1968 as a private yacht for Fredrick Parks of Boston Deepsea Fisheries. The hull was built in the BIM shipyard in Killybegs, County Donegal, then, with engines installed, she was towed to Malahide, County Dublin for fitting out. At that stage, she was named Lammermuir. Once sea trials were completed, Parks took delivery. She was renamed "Judith Parks", after his wife, and was sailed to Grimsby, which was to be her first homeport.

Over several years, she alternated between Grimsby and the Mediterranean. On one such journey, while crossing the Bay of Biscay in heavy seas, the skipper spotted two drifting life rafts, whose occupants were the survivors of two French fishing boats that had collided and sunk while they were pair trawling. Having picked up the sailors, the Judith Parks sailed to their local port and delivered them home with much celebration. Around ten years later, Parks' wife died. He sold the vessel and she was renamed Salutay.

We bought the vessel in 1988 at Shamrock Quay, Southampton and sailed her to Phillips Boatyard in Dartmouth for a major refit. In 1989 we sailed back to Strangford Lough in Northern Ireland and began our first season operating as a charter vessel running liveaboard diving trips to the Isle of Man and Rathlin Island on the North coast of Ireland.

And the rest, as they say, is history.

2. Finding the Big 3: by Al

The Audacious

For a long time, I had heard stories about the WW1 and WW2 convoy battles and shipwrecks off the coast of Malin Head, the most northern point on Ireland's coastline and a natural choke point between Ireland and Scotland's North Channel through which all shipping has to pass to reach the port of Liverpool.

As a teenager in the late 1980s, while I was diving the wreck of the RMS Laurentic, mined off the entrance to Lough Swilly, just west of Malin Head, my dive buddy Mike McGinn told me about another WW1 wreck further offshore, the Super Dreadnought Battleship, HMS Audacious. I asked where it was and if it had been dived. He told me that it was further offshore in deep water and un-dived. With that glimmer of information, a seed was sown.

Several years later, I was aboard Salutay, we were sailing off the coast of Northern Ireland and we had a group of bird watchers on board, who wanted to count specific species of pelagic seabirds that lived and fed further offshore. After looking at the chart of Malin Head and the surrounding waters, I pinpointed a group of wreck marks that I was interested in locating. Among them I hoped to find the Audacious.

So, while they counted birds, I hunted wrecks. We steamed west and further north, trailing a smelly concoction of cornflakes and fish oil in our wake. I watched the video screen of the echo sounder as we closed in on the wreck markers. Meanwhile there were shouts from the upper deck of "Wilson's petrels to starboard" and "fulmars on the port beam!". Approximately 15 miles north of Lough Swilly, in roughly the last position of HMS Audacious, the trace on the echo sounder began to grow and eventually rose up to a height of over 13m off the seabed. Could this be the great battleship?

At the end of the day I had a list of sites I wanted to dive and the bird watchers had a list of seabirds that they'd identified and counted. Everyone was happy. The first mark on my list was the one I hoped would turn out to be HMS Audacious. The Salutay was tied up the following week and the weather was looking favourable, so I called on my friend and dive buddy Simon Bamford, who owned a 7.5m RIB fitted with all manner of wreck location tools. Because of the depth, I chose to dive trimix, which would reduce my narcosis. Earlier that year I had spent some time doing trimix diver training in Key West, Florida under Capt. Billy Deans, an early mixed gas diving pioneer.

Technical diving in the UK was still in its infancy and there were very few UK divers trained to dive on trimix. One of them happened to be my friend Dave Rigg. I phoned him, explained what I had found and wanted to do and we put a plan together.

On the day of the dive the weather gods smiled upon us. We had calm seas and sunshine. We launched from Lough Swilly and made the transit to the dive site in under an hour, thanks to a large 200hp fuel-guzzling outboard engine. With the wreck located and a shot line dropped on the highest point, we prepared to enter the water. I was using a set of

double 120s filled with trimix 17/40 and two side-slung decompression cylinders containing EAN36 and pure oxygen respectively. We planned for a 25-minute bottom time at 63m, giving us a total dive time of 96 minutes.

As I went down the shot-line, the clear blue Atlantic water slowly turned darker and at around 36m, I started to make out a dark shape appearing below me. I touched down on the top of a large hull at around 50m. In the distance, amidst shoals of pollock, lurked something very big. As I swam closer, a huge three-bladed high-speed propeller emerged from the gloom, followed by a set of double rudders and three more high speed propellers. From my research, I knew that this was a typical Super Dreadnought stern design and as the Audacious was the only vessel of this type recorded as having been sunk off Malin Head, this had to be her.

I decided to turn around and swim towards the bow to see what else I could discover. I swam along the hull and there before me lay a mass of destruction with twisted metal everywhere, the result of the magazine explosion that had occurred while the ship was under tow after hitting a mine during gunnery practice.

I got closer to a break in the wreckage where I swam over large warheads from the main armament and smaller 4-inch guns that were scattered around on the seabed. Reaching the break, I could see below me in the distance a large barbette on which the massive turret had been seated. Beyond was the turret itself, upside down on the sea floor. Dropping onto the seabed, I swam towards the huge pair of 13.5-inch gun barrels that poked ominously out. With the main armament identified, the wreck before me could not be any other than HMS Audacious.

I took a quick glance at my bottom timer: my 25 minutes were nearly up. It was time to leave. I deployed my delayed surface marker buoy and started my ascent. My first decompression stop and gas switch was at 33m and it would be over an hour before I reached the surface. The dive had been a complete success but this was not the end of the season's wreck hunting.

The Justicia

Not long afterwards, I set about looking for another worthy target. The one shipwreck that jumped out beyond anything else on the north coast of Ireland was the Royal Mail Ship (RMS) Justicia.

The Justicia had been located several years before and was a popular offshore fishing site. I had the latitude and longitude from the early eighties, when one of the fishing skippers had positioned our day boat Ocean Vaux over the site. As far as I knew, the wreck had never been dived. She lay in 70m, which was beyond air limits but well within trimix range.

She lay over twenty nautical miles from our anchorage in Lough Swilly, so settled weather and calm seas were required. On the chosen day, the conditions were ideal. We arrived at the wreck site and quickly located the Justicia on the echo sounder. There she was, sitting at 70m and rising 6m from the seabed.

For this dive I again had my Genesis twinset filled with trimix 17/40 and two decompression mixes of nitrox 36 and 100% oxygen. Due to the vast size of the ship, I took my Aquazepp underwater scooter so that I could cover more of the wreck in the time available.

As I was on my scooter I would be diving solo, I jumped in and after a quick check of my equipment at 6m I motored down the shot line in the clear Atlantic water. At around 45m, I could see the Justicia spread out below me. A massive boiler came into view between shoals of pollock. The shot was just forward of the collapsed bridge but, with the good visibility, I could see the bow section in the distance, sitting proud of a small debris field. I selected a faster speed on my AquaZepp and headed off towards the bow. Where the forward bulkhead had broken off, I could see down several decks. Near the large anchor winch, steam capstans were pushed up through the deck. I cruised past the bow, stopped the Aquazepp and looked back. What an amazing sight! The bow was virtually intact with an anchor still in its hawse pipe.

Unfortunately I was approaching the end of my planned bottom time, but I still had more to see, so I turned up the Aquazepp a little more and sped off for the stern. On the way, I passed over at least six massive boilers, then the engines and lots of flattened superstructure covered with portholes and square windows. The ship seemed to go on and on but eventually I reached the stern where I was greeted with the sight of a large propeller sticking out of the sand. I checked my bottom timer and contents gauge. Twenty-five minutes had elapsed so it was time to go up.

I deployed my delayed surface marker buoy, ascended to my first stop at 33m and switched to nitrox 36. The next 80 minutes of decompression were spent reliving the dive and trying to wrap my mind around the sheer size of the Justicia. Many more dives on the Justicia would follow.

The Empire Heritage

When you discover a shipwreck and dive it for the first time there is a great deal of anticipation. All sorts of thoughts run through your head. How intact is it? Is it upright or capsized? Has it been dived before? Will the bell be there? But nothing prepared me for what I was about to find when I first dived the Empire Heritage. Not in my wildest dreams did I expect to find a cargo of Sherman tanks!

Already in 1994, I had located and found HMS Audacious and had also dived the RMS Justicia for the first time. I knew where the Empire Heritage and the MV Pinto were. They were less than a mile apart and had been located in the 1960s by HMS Bulldog during an Admiralty survey. As far as I was aware, neither had ever been dived.

The Empire Heritage was built in 1930 in Newcastle upon Tyne. She was formerly called the Tafelberg and had operated as a whaling factory ship. The German U-boat U-482

torpedoed her en route from New York to Liverpool and she sank with the loss of 113 lives. At the time, she was carrying a cargo of 16000 tons of fuel oil and 1900 tons of deck cargo including the Sherman tanks.

The Salutay was chartered for a neap week in July and we were lucky to have a light southwesterly wind and very little swell. We quickly found the wreck. She was resting at 67m and sat over 6m proud of the seabed. One of her loading "goal-post" masts was as shallow as 47m. Again, my dive buddy was Dave Rigg, and again, for this dive, we were on our usual bottom gas of 17/40 trimix, with nitrox 36 and pure oxygen for decompression. As we went down the shot, the wreck came into view at around 45m and the first things I spotted between the shoals of pollock were the "goal-post" loading masts and a variety of strange objects scattered on the deck and seabed.

We touched bottom and trimmed out, then I swam towards the hold. Sticking out from it was a turret with a short gun barrel. I looked around and saw another upturned Sherman tank with its caterpillar tracks clearly visible. Looking around, I noticed several more tanks were scattered on the seabed, along with a truck. Dave and I checked our gauges and swam forward over an accommodation module and towards the bridge. I spotted a large telegraph and made for that, while Dave headed over to the left. The telegraph was jammed under a large beam and freeing it would require some work. I started shifting debris.

Then I heard a noise and looked over to where Dave was frantically gesturing at me to come over. He had found the ship's bell. It was securely attached to a six-foot goose neck bar and was sticking out beneath another girder, Dave bashed the nut and bolt securing the bell but to no avail. I managed to move the girder with my crowbar but the steel bar was too heavy. We needed a hacksaw and we didn't have one.

Our bottom time was running out, as was our bottom gas after all this exertion. So we dragged the bell and bell fixtures under a nearby steel plate so they were out of sight. We began our ascent and, at 33m, switched to nitrox 36. At 27m, we deployed our deco

markers and line and started the slow process of decompression. After 106 minutes in the water we climbed the ladder back on to the Salutay and immediately began planning to return to the Empire Heritage, properly tooled up this time, and recover the bell.

The Bell Recovery

I had a week to recover the bell before the next Salutay charter. Dave could not stick around so it was up to me. I called Simon Bamford, whose RIB I had used earlier in the year for the first Audacious dive. He and his RIB were both available, as was Kim Cox, another trimix diver.

We launched from Lough Swilly and were soon scooting across the wave-tops at 30 knots. There was a definite air of excitement and anticipation among our small team. We arrived at the wreck site and Simon dropped the shot as close to the bridge as he could. The plan was that I would go in first, unclip the shot, send it up with a lift-bag, then swim the shot line to the bell location and secure it. Then I would start work with a large hacksaw on the steel pipe, while Simon tied the RIB into the line.

I dropped in and was soon on the bottom. Luckily, the shot was not far from the bell so I quickly bagged up the shot and swam the shot line over. I dragged the bell and steel pipe from under the plate where we had stashed it and began working on it with the hacksaw. After 25 minutes the bell was nearly free but it still needed another 5 minutes work. I was getting low on bottom mix and had reached the end of my planned bottom time so I had to ascend.

As we had planned, after 30 minutes Simon came down past me on the shot line to finish the job. Ten minutes later, while I was still decompressing, the bell flew by me towards the surface, attached to a lift-bag, clipped into the shot line: mission accomplished. When

I surfaced I removed my kit, climbed into the RIB and there it was, the Empire Heritage's bell. I scraped some of the shells and barnacles away and made out the inscription "TAFELBERG", her original name. I started cleaning it up while Kim took my Aquazepp for a tour of the wreck and Simon decompressed on the shot line.

On our return to port, I declared the bell to the Receiver of Wrecks for posterity and, the following week, the Salutay returned to the Empire Heritage with a group of technical divers called "The Bandits" and we recovered the bridge telegraph. It had been a memorable wreck diving season.

3. Other Malin Head Wrecks: by Al

The U-89

The majority of U-boat wrecks off Malin Head are submarines that were scuttled as part of Operation Deadlight, so it made quite a change for us to dive on an operational loss from WW1. On 12 February 1918, the U-89 was on patrol 24 miles north of Malin Head when she was located and heavily depth charged. She surfaced, was rammed by HMS Roxburgh and quickly sank. There were no survivors.

My friend Michael McVeigh was based in Downings, Co. Donegal and owned a day boat, which he chartered out to divers and fishermen. While fishing, he located the wreck, got a dive team together and dived and identified the U-89. I heard about this, contacted him

and he was kind enough to give me the location. All we needed then was a trip with divers capable of diving her and a decent spell of weather. The U-89 lies quite a distance offshore, around four miles north of the Justicia, but sits on a bank, which rises to 60m. Otherwise she would be in much deeper water.

As luck would have it, a few weeks later I had a group capable of making the dive. They had booked the Salutay for a week to dive the classics: HMS Audacious, Empire Heritage and RMS Justicia and, when I told them about the U-89, they were more than keen. During this trip I was completing a closed-circuit trimix course for two divers and this dive was to be their final qualifying dive. So, as we all descended, I was armed with my PD100 video camera to film the divers' trim and technique.

The U-89 was shotted just in front of the conning tower, which was still intact. You could look down into the conning tower and clearly see the open hatch giving access to the control room. Directly in front of the conning tower a huge 105mm deck gun pointed menacingly over the bow. Not far from the gun the forward torpedo-loading hatch lay open, allowing a view of the torpedoes secured in their racks. The bow casing had corroded, exposing the pressure hull, and one of the bow torpedo tubes lay open with a live torpedo sticking out of it.

As we started to swim towards the conning tower, I was filming my students and suddenly a massive sunfish swam in front of the conning tower. Luckily, I caught it on camera. It turned out to be a great bit of footage. We then swam aft and, directly behind the conning tower, spotted the unmistakeable evidence of the ramming by HMS Roxburgh. There was a huge gash cut through the pressure hull, exposing both diesel engines. Without doubt the U-89 would have sunk very quickly, allowing little chance for the crew to escape: quite a sobering thought!

A stern-mounted 88mm deck gun was also visible, but both propellers and hydroplanes were covered in fishing net. The sunfish made a brief second swim-by and disappeared. After 30 minutes, it was time to go up, so we deployed our delayed surface marker buoys and started our slow ascent.

On board the Salutay that evening, we reviewed the footage of this amazing dive and remarked on how lucky we had been to share it with a giant sunfish.

SS Roscommon

This wreck was originally known as the Slate Wreck and was found by Michael McVeigh on his dive vessel the Rosguill. I first dived it with him, then started to dive it from the Salutay, along with the wreck of the SS Devonian nearby.

The SS Roscommon was built in Workman Clarks shipyard in Belfast in 1902 and weighed 8238 tons. Her original name was the Oswestry Grange. On 21 August 1917, she was en route from Manchester to Australia with general cargo and was sunk by the U-53 around twenty miles northeast of Tory Island. There were no casualties. She now lies in about 78m and only sits a few metres off the seabed.

On my first dive on the wreck I took my video camera. Even on trimix, I found that, after a deep dive, I would review the footage and spot things I hadn't seen during the dive so it was very useful. This was in the early 2000s and at this time I was using a Buddy Inspiration Rebreather that allowed me to dive deeper, use less gas and have a more efficient decompression, compared with open circuit diving. The rebreather proved to be a great tool for deep diving and wreck exploration.

Arriving on the wreck, I was rewarded with the sort of great visibility you always hope to get off the north coast of Ireland; 20m in natural light. This was at nearly 80m. Most of the hull was flattened into the seabed and well broken up, but everywhere I looked I could see piles of slate, which had no doubt formed a large part of the general cargo. The shot

was close to a large boiler sitting proud on the seabed and looking further aft I could make out three more boilers. I swam forward over more piles of slate neatly packed in what was left of the holds and then came across a consignment of china. I had a quick root around to see if there were any nice pieces; then carried on towards the bow.

The bow was the highest point on the wreck. It had broken off from the main hull but was still intact. It was at 90 degrees to the seabed and pointed towards the surface. A hatch was open on the forecastle and I peered inside, but could see nothing of interest. As I swam around the bow, I saw a huge anchor still sitting in its hawse pipe, its size giving a good idea of how large this ship once was.

Dave Rigg joined me there, astride his Aquazepp scooter, and we started a systematic search for the ship's bell. Unfortunately, we didn't find it. I swam back towards the shot line and boilers and started my ascent. It was definitely time to leave. My bottom time had been 30 minutes and, even with the rebreather, I had accumulated 100 minutes of decompression.

SS Devonian

The Devonian was built by Harland and Wolff shipyard in Belfast and weighed 10418 tons. On 21 August 1917, she was on passage from Liverpool to Boston when she was torpedoed by the U-53, the same U-boat that had sunk the SS Roscommon earlier that day. The two shipwrecks are only just over one mile apart. I first dived the Devonian in June 2003, again thanks to Michael McVeigh, who gave me the co-ordinates. The Devonian turned out to be a little larger and more intact than the Roscommon and lay listed on her port side. She was also better fitted out, with higher quality brass fixtures. On my first dive on her I managed to bag up a very nice circular, flush-mounted deck light that was made of high quality bronze. This was a bonus, as a lot of the portholes and windows were still well secured. I swam around the bow, which had broken off and was lying on its port side. A huge anchor was still in place in the hawse pipe and there was an open hatch that allowed access to the forecastle. I dropped to the seabed and looked back towards the bow, marvelling at the impressive sight before me.

SS Boniface

The Boniface is one of the more unusual shipwrecks we dive on the north coast of Ireland mainly because of her cargo of copper ingots. She was built in 1904 by Barclay Curle and Company in Glasgow as a passenger / cargo vessel and was operated by the Booth Steamship Company in Liverpool. She weighed in at 3506 tons. On 23 August 1917, she was torpedoed 7 miles northeast of Arranmore Island by U-53 while under passage from New York to the Clyde. Two people lost their lives. In the 1960s the wreck was heavily salvaged and grabs on the end of cranes were used to recover the copper ingots. They removed the majority of the cargo but some ingots were left behind, easy pickings for a diver with a 65kg liftbag! I first dived this wreck in 1999 with a mixed group of rebreather and open circuit divers. Those on rebreathers had the advantage of a helium-based diluent while the open circuit divers had to use air. The Boniface lay in around 52 metres so it wasn't beyond reach for air divers. I dived with two other rebreather divers Ken and Alison Farrow. Freda jumped in with us on a twinset of air. We descended and Freda quickly overtook us. She was negatively buoyant with her 300-bar, 7-litre twinset and reached the bottom in about a minute. We arrived a few minutes later, clear-headed thanks to our helium mixes, to find Freda completely narked after her rapid descent. I gave her the OK signal and she responded but her eyes were like soup bowls. Much to her annoyance, I signalled that she should go back up the shot line, which she did.

Most of the Boniface was flattened from the salvage, but both of her boilers were still in place and, in the holds, toblerone-shaped copper ingots could be prised out from below steel plates and girders. I managed to bag up four ingots: not a bad haul. Since this dive I've been back to the Boniface twice. All but a few hard-to-reach ingots have gone, no doubt recovered by other enterprising divers.

4. Memories of Malin: by Freda

SS Laurentic

The SS Laurentic was a British ocean liner of the White Star Line. She was converted to an armed merchant cruiser at the onset of WW I and sank after striking two mines north of

Ireland on 25 January 1917, with the loss of 354 lives. She was carrying about 43 tons of gold ingots at the time of her loss and, as of 2017, 20 gold bars have yet to be recovered. She is a very popular recreational dive as the maximum depth is usually 40m, or less depending on tides, and there is often clear blue water around the wreck. The Laurentic

also makes for a great back up dive when the conditions prevent you from getting out to dive the deeper Malin Head wrecks.

The Laurentic is one of my favourite dives off Malin because its comparatively shallow depth means you can spend plenty of time on it. I know every inch of the wreck because I have dived it so many times. I often used to give guided tours so that divers would not miss the highlights, such as the bow and guns. One gun stands magnificently upright as if it is waiting to be loaded.

The Laurentic has six boilers, which lie close to one another, apart from the sixth boiler, which lies on its own just off the wreck not far from the starboard gunwales. About three quarters of the way up, just under a section of the gunwales there is an outcrop of white parozoanthus anemones. They look almost like real flowers. These are my marker for the shot line as Al usually drops the shot here, unless he drops it on the bow.

I once found the Laurentic's safe shortly after it had been re-discovered, but sadly no gold! The ship's bell now hangs in a church in Port Salon. I would scooter around the Laurentic from time to time when Al had his Aquazepp on board. Scootering gives you a whole new perspective. Just being that little bit higher off the wreck makes the dive feel completely different and of course it is great fun.

Argo Delos

The Argo Delos was a Greek motor vessel out of Piraeus bound from Glasgow to load sugar for China. One mile north of Inishtrahull Island at Tor Beg on 22 October 1960, she hit an isolated rock, ran aground, broke in two and sank.

The bow section lies in a gully at Tor Rocks. The stern section with the complete engine room was salvaged but, while it was being towed, it sank (again) 4.5 miles northeast of Glengad Head. It now lies intact at a maximum depth of 46m, with the top at 33m. She is a great wreck so I would dive her whenever I got the chance. Al would always place the shot near the upturned keel of the hull. She is upside down and large sections of hull are intact, so it is tricky to navigate around her. There is a huge swimthrough to the engine room, which is always filled with shoals of saithe and pollock. You can go through to the other side, which takes you out and around the back towards the stern to where the propeller lies half-buried in the seabed. The dive always involves a lot of swimming, but there is plenty to see and the visibility is always excellent. Near the break, remnants of the main mast and radar scanner can still be seen, along with deck cargo and assorted machinery.

Although the wreck is ideal for penetration, you have to be careful when you swim through the engine room not to get globules of heavy oil on your dive kit. When you are on your decompression stops, you often see globules of oil bubbling past you to the surface and, at slack water, small patches of heavy oil on the surface mark the site.

A Lonely Dolphin

I remember one time on the way back from Malin to Donegal heading for Port Rush, It was a calm day and one of the divers spotted two dolphins. One was not moving and we eventually realised that it was dead. The other dolphin was swimming around and around it, as if trying to save it. It looked so helpless: such a sad sight.

Sunfish on the Audacious

I was diving with Al one time on the wreck of the Audacious, back when we had a third crewman and he was a skipper: "the good old days", as Al says. The visibility was a little cloudy but, as we swam from the guns to the stern, I spotted a humongous sunfish at least 2m across. We both just gazed at it in awe. Under water they look so graceful. They have beautiful large wide eyes and the skin is as shiny as polished silver. The sunfish just glided slowly past us without a care, completely unbothered by our presence.

5. Operation Deadlight U-Boats: by Al

Operation Deadlight was the Royal Navy's disposal of 116 German submarines off the North Ireland coast in 1945 and 1946. They had surrendered at the end of WW2 and had to be sunk. The operation was not entirely successful and half of the submarines being towed to the official dumping area foundered en-route. In 2001-3, aboard Salutay, we set out to find, dive and record as many of the U-boats as we could. In all we looked at 14 wrecks which included a number of historic examples. U155 had a successful career and U2511 and U2506 were new Type XXI boats. They were great trips, made all the more special for being able to work with Al and Freda. Great friends, special times.

Dr Innes McCartney, 2017

In July 2001, Innes McCartney chartered us for two weeks of diving and searching off Malin Head for lost U-boats, which were part of Operation Deadlight. Our aim was to locate and dive on any boats we could find that were at depths of less than 100m.

U-778

During the expedition we located many Type VIIC U-boats. These were the most common class of U-boat and designed to be front line North Atlantic vessels. Because there were so many of them, we nicknamed them "Ford Fiestas".

The U-778 is one of these. She lies on a sandy seabed in 67m and without doubt this was the most intact U-boat any of us had ever dived on. The bow section was still intact, as was the outer hull, and both bow hydroplanes were still in place. This is very rare as, in our experience, the outer cladding normally falls off leaving the pressure hull and bow caps exposed. A schnorchel was visible recessed into the deck and you could still see the coating of radar absorbing material on the head. It was fantastic: from bow tip to stern, everything was there.

In my opinion, the reason there was so little damage to her superstructure was because she lay in line with the prevailing currents.

U-155

Locating and diving the U-155 was one of main goals of the expedition. The U-155 was a type IXC boat and was commanded by Adolf Piening, the man who sank the escort aircraft carrier HMS Avenger. It was also he who devised a safer route across the Bay of Biscay to avoid allied aircraft and this was nicknamed the "Piening Route".

We found the U155 in 75m, sitting upright on an even keel. Her forward hydroplanes and torpedo tubes had fallen off, revealing the pressure hull but apart from this damage, the rest of the boat was virtually intact. The schnorchel was in place on the starboard side of the foredeck and the heavy reinforcing for the anti-aircraft gun mountings around the conning tower was visible. The conning tower hatch was open, which allowed us to peer down into the control room. The type IXC boats were much wider than the common VIIC boats, which looked almost like canoes in comparison.

U-2511 Elektroboot

This was one of the Deadlight boats that we had found before the trip. Of the many shipwrecks we have found off Malin Head over the years, it was one of the most surprising. At the time, we were looking for the HMS Authesua, a British destroyer, and my dive buddy Simon Bamford had some marks that he wanted to check out. Once again we used his RIB and Dave Rigg and Stuart Adams were again diving with us.

We launched from Lough Swilly and swiftly motored out to our target over 23 miles offshore. Once on site we started to circle the estimated position slowly, but our echo sounder detected no wreckage. So Simon deployed our secret weapon, a proton magnetometer. A magnetometer is basically an underwater metal detector with a transceiver (tow fish), which we towed along 50m behind the RIB travelling at a slow speed. The model we had was a Planet MX500. At the time, it was pretty much the state of the art, as it linked into our GPS plotter, giving us an accurate position of any targets found.

The magnetometer was calibrated to the local area we were searching in and would detect any unusually large amounts of iron and show the location on the display. Operating and interpreting the data from a magnetometer is a bit of a black art and takes lots of practice but luckily Simon is a dab hand and within 30 minutes he found something he thought might be a shipwreck. We switched the echo sounder on again, made some slow speed runs over the area and quickly located a target, over half a mile from where we had started our search. It sat in 70m and rose about 5m above the seabed. On the echo sounder, it looked fairly large and intact. Once we were over the wreck, I deployed the shot and shot line, then we quickly checked our dive gear and kitted up.

As usual in this sort of depth, we were using trimix 17/40 and nitrox 36 and 100% oxygen for decompression. Also as usual, the Atlantic waters this far offshore were crystal clear and, from around 35m, a shape of a shipwreck started to reveal itself to us. To our surprise this was no destroyer: it was a U-boat, but a much bigger U-boat than we had ever seen or dived on. It was a type XXI U-boat known as an Elektroboot. These were built towards the end of WW 2 but never used in combat.

The type XXI was a revolutionary design with a streamlined hull and conning tower and a larger than normal battery bank, which allowed longer submerged time and greater underwater speed than any other submarine at that time. It was fitted with a schnorchel so it could recharge its batteries with the main diesel engines drawing air via the schnorchel at periscope depth, meaning it would never have to surface and risk detection.

The sub was lying slightly on her side with some shell holes in her conning tower, but it was otherwise fully intact. As we swam over the streamlined conning tower, the anti-aircraft turrets with 20 mm guns were visible at either end. The schnorchel was broken off and lying on the seabed. We swam towards the bow passing the forward torpedo-loading hatch and dropped down onto the bright white sand. Looking back at the menacing bow, we could see all six torpedo tubes and the streamlined hull stretching into the distance.

U-2506

Our records showed us that there was a second Type XXI to find, the U-2506, and we found her on the last day of our trip, much closer inshore than we had been working. We only had one more wreck to dive and we assumed it would be another VIIC, but what a pleasant surprise it was to find a big Type XXI instead. The U-2506 lies in 66m of water and is virtually as intact as the U-778. The 20mm gun barrels are still in place on both turrets and the fin is in fantastic condition. The schnorchel and periscopes are still intact as well: definitely one of the best U-Boat wrecks I have ever dived.

6. Tory Island: by Freda

Tory (officially known by its Irish name *Toraigh*), is an island 9 miles off the northwest coast of County Donegal in Ulster, Ireland, and is the most remote inhabited island of Ireland. Our north coast of Ireland Malin Head charters always included a visit to Tory to dive two spectacular sites.

Tornadrallagh

This is a 25-to-30m deep gully in the cliff-face with huge granite boulders strewn over a cobbled seabed, sheer sea-cliffs carpeted with jewel anemones, and arches cut by the tide. With the usual 30m-plus visibility, it is just mind-blowing. It takes 30 minutes to swim through the gully. On your return you can swim shallower if your air is getting low.

Marnid Rock

This is a dive that starts at the cliff wall and then opens up over a wide expanse of seabed dotted with boulders covered in jewel anemones of every colour imaginable. It is like swimming through companionways in a shipwreck formed from boulders and rocks that you cannot see over the top of. Shoals of schooling mackerel are always a treat to see above you. I have seen sunfish here quite often and one time I was diving here with my sister and we saw a pair of sunfish! Not quite as big as the one Al and I saw on HMS Audacious but seeing two together was a rare treat. Of course my sister Julie thought I saw pairs of sunfish all the time. I decided not to disappoint her and said, "of course I do".

7. RMS Lusitania: by Al

The best projects normally come out of the blue with little warning. It was November 2003 and we had just finished our season of long weekend charters out of Oban on the West Coast of Scotland when I received this email inquiry.

It was from Greg Bemis, an American who owned the wreck of the ill-fated passenger liner RMS Lusitania. He was inquiring if we were available for charter to dive the wreck in June the following year.

The Lusitania had been on my wish list for a long time. I had come close to diving it in 1996 on a project organised by Kevin Gurr, but due to bad weather and poor timing I missed out by one day. So I was definitely keen for this new charter to go ahead.

The Lusitania was a famous Cunard Liner that was torpedoed by the German U-boat U-20 on 7 May 1915. The unprovoked sinking of this vessel turned public opinion in many countries against Germany and contributed to the entry of the USA into WW 1. The wreck lies 11 miles off the Old Head of Kinsale in Southern Ireland, at the opposite end of Ireland from where we normally operated, so the charter meant we had to cover quite some sea miles to get there.

Once contact was made with Greg, we agreed on the charter rate and he told me what he hoped to achieve during the week. He planned to dive the wreck himself, which would be no mean feat, given that she was lying at 93m and he was 71 years old. He told me not to worry as his instructor was coming along to keep an eye on him. His instructor turned out to be Hal Watts, the former holder of the deep air diving record, who had just turned 69. Not to be put off, I immediately started to work out how to run this dive as safely as possible for my two elderly clients.

First of all, due to the depth of the wreck, a long amount of decompression would be required. So, to make this more safe and comfortable, I would build a trapeze-like decompression station to allow the divers to rest during their long stops at 9m, 6m and 4.5m. Greg also wanted his dive to the Lusitania to be filmed so I recruited my long time friend and professional underwater cameraman Dan Burton to do the job.

The time went fast and soon it was June. A fully-fuelled-and-supplied MV Salutay set sail from Bangor, Northern Ireland on a 30-hour transit to the beautiful natural harbour of Kinsale in Cork, where we welcomed our eager divers on board.

We needed to do a checkout dive and equipment familiarisation and we picked the WW 2 wreck of the U-260 U-boat in 40m. I gave Greg and Hal 12-litre 300-bar twinsets, which held lots of gas but were very heavy. When I saw them kitting themselves out with weight belts, I advised them that they would not need any weight beyond the cylinders but they told me they preferred to dive heavy as this would allow them to descend feet first to the wreck. This was a new concept to me and I took it with a pinch of salt.

I shotted the wreck, deployed the decompression station and got the safety divers into the water. Then I watched anxiously from the deck with my drysuit on, ready to enter the water after Greg and Hal, who were kitting up. Their twinsets were filled with nitrox 28 and they also carried two stage cylinders, one with nitrox 40, the other with nitrox 80.

In they jumped and down they went, rapidly passing Dan the camera man at 30m and arriving on the wreck at record time, grossly over weighted. Luckily they had high volume BCDS to compensate for the extra lead and allow them to maintain neutral buoyancy during their swim around the wreck. With the dive over, they came up the shot line and crossed over onto the decompression station without incident under the watchful eye of Freda, who was our roving safety diver.

Back on board the Salutay a post dive debrief was held and, much to my relief, they decided wisely to dispense with the weight belts for the Lusitania dive. After that, all we needed was a weather window and a quick look at the weather forecast showed strong southwest winds. So, like any good diver, we retired to the local pub to await calmer seas.

The opportunity to dive the wreck came a few days later, when a 6-hour weather window appeared on the forecast. This was exactly what we were waiting for. So early that morning we set sail. Among the crew was an official from the Irish National Heritage department to oversee that we stuck to the strict rules in our diving permit, which did not allow any artefacts to be removed from the protected wreck site.

As the Lusitania is an extremely large vessel and scattered over a vast area, it would not be possible to see the complete wreck in one dive, so Greg asked that I shot the stern section. This area was known to be free of nets at that time. We arrived on site ahead of

slack water and were rewarded with calm seas and blue skies. The wreck was rapidly shotted and the decompression station was deployed. The plan was that my dive partner Gary Sharp and I were to descend first to double-check that there were no nets present. If all looked safe, we would deploy a floating pellet to signal that the dive could begin.

I was diving at the time with a Buddy Inspiration that would give me a longer bottom time on the wreck and a more efficient decompression. Gary was diving open-circuit with a monster twinset of 20 litre tanks and multiple decompression stage cylinders, so gas supply would not be an issue for him. We descended effortlessly through the clear Atlantic water and, at 75m, saw the Lusitania laid out below us in all directions. Thankfully, the stern area was indeed net-free so I deployed the pellet.

Gary and I explored the stern section, which was well broken up due to depth charging in WW 2. Three of the four propellers were missing, having been salvaged by Oceaneering International in 1982. After our 25-minute bottom time, we waved goodbye to "Lucy" and ascended. At our first decompression stop at 50m we were passed by Greg and Hal descending rapidly feet first and cameraman Dan finning like mad to keep up! Now began the nervous wait for them to ascend.

When the team reached the wreck Hal attached a light to the shot line to help Greg stay in sight of it. Greg then dropped onto a piece of wreckage and, while Dan was filming,

removed his regulator and kissed the wreck. He had achieved his life-long ambition to dive the Lusitania. Not wanting to out-stay his welcome, he began his ascent up the shot line straight away.

As I floated next to the 6m bar on the decompression station, I was relieved to see the team coming back up towards me. Once they were all on the trapeze, Freda broke the station free and we drifted effortlessly in the clear water for our decompression. I looked across at Greg and he gave me an OK signal and a huge beam of a smile: mission accomplished.

8. The Isle of Man: by Freda

When we operated from Scotland, first from Portpatrick and then out of Stranraer, we ran trips to the Isle of Man. We also used it as a back up plan if we could not get to or dive the north coast of Ireland. The Isle of Man offers fantastic recreational diving in amazing clear

blue water. We saw an untold amount of baskers while we were operating there. Here are brief details of some of the wrecks and a couple of other top sites.

The Thracian

The Thracian sank behind the Isle of Man while under-tow to Liverpool to be fitted out. The rigging was never completed and, sadly, the Thracian never sailed. The Thracian was of all-steel construction, with a hull of steel plates over steel frames, so there is a lot of intact hull standing up from the seabed, albeit upside-down. The highest point is the stern, rising to 29m from the seabed at 36m. Huge steel masts are stretched out on the seabed. The visibility isn't always that great, due to silt, but when conditions are good it is a lovely interesting dive and the edges of the wreck are great for scalloping.

The SS Liverpool

The SS Liverpool sank after hitting a mine in 1916. She lies about 18 nautical miles southeast of the Isle of Man. She sits upright and is fairly intact. Al would usually drop the shot on the starboard side of the stern, where anemones and hydroids cover the outer ring of the steering quadrant. Originally, there was another deck level but this has collapsed. There are the remains of a bearing near the top of the rudderpost. A magnificent four-bladed iron propeller is still in place and the rudder is set hard to port and also covered in plumose and daisy anemones. There is always a shoal of bib or pout whiting somewhere around. The seabed is at around 38m here. Every time I have dived the Liverpool, the visibility has been fantastic. It is possible to view the whole wreck in one dive too. There not much in the way of penetration opportunity as it is a very open wreck, but it is great for photographers.

The Fire King

On 10 December 1939, the Fire King, a vessel of just over 700 tons, with a length of 58m and beam of 10m and powered by a triple-expansion steam engine, was bound for Glasgow with a general cargo. Approaching the Point of Ayre on a fine, clear morning, the ship spotted the mail steamer Duke of Lancaster ahead of her, on its way from Belfast to Heysham with cargo and around 180 passengers. The ships were on a collision course, but for some reason the Duke of Lancaster failed to give way. The bows of the larger ship sliced right through the second hold of the Fire King at about 3.30pm and the Fire King sank within minutes. The Ramsey lifeboat attended the collision scene with a doctor on board and the survivors were put ashore at Ramsey. In 1940 the exact position of the Fire King was identified, the ship was salvaged and then blown up so that it would not be an obstruction to shipping. The Fire King is a fabulous little dive site, teeming with sea life everywhere you turn. The stern is still largely intact with boilers and wreckage scattered around. Due to its location in the middle of two fierce tidal streams, it is probably the most colourful wreck around the Island. It usually has a very small tidal window and you can only dive it on neaps. Again, here we generally always had great visibility.

The Sugar Loaf Caves

I used to love diving these caves although they are not true caves, being open to the air at the top. The site is just 10 to 15m deep and only 2 miles from Port St Mary, so it makes a perfect second dive of the day. The walls of the caves are carpeted in jewel anemones.

Chicken Rock

Chicken Rock is an isolated pinnacle marked by an impressive lighthouse with a diving depth range of 20 to 45m. Strong currents and over-falls sometimes make the conditions interesting if you time it wrong. We only ever put experienced divers in here. It is a fantastic drift dive, teeming with life and colour.

The Romeo

The Romeo was a 1730-ton, defensively armed, British merchant steamer. In March 1918, just 7 miles south of the Mull of Galloway, she was torpedoed by a submarine without warning and sank. Twenty-nine lives were lost. The Romeo lies in around 46m and is broken in half. The bow section lies on its port side and is very broken up. Visibility can often be poor due to the muddy seabed, but sometimes you get lucky and we have had over 10m of visibility on occasion. But the chance of poor visibility doesn't take away from the fact that this is a great wreck. It sits 8m proud of the seabed and is bristling with fish and other marine life. It is possible to swim both halves of the 150m-long wreck in one dive. But it's easier to do that with a scooter!

9. Rathlin and Fair Head: by Freda & Al

Rathlin Island is Northern Ireland's most northerly inhabited island and is located 15 miles from Scotland's Mull of Kintyre. The island is shaped like an L in reverse and measures 4 miles by 2.5 miles. Rathlin's highest point is Slieveard at 134m above sea level and it has a steadily growing population of around 150.

The Loughgarry: by Freda

On a recreational charter, Rathlin Island was always high on our list to dive, with the wreck of the Loughgarry one of the main attractions. She was a ferry that was working as a troop ship when she sank in WW 2. After encountering bad weather whilst heading for the Mull of Kintyre, she struck the rocks and finally sank on 21 January 1942. She lies in 33m on the east coast of Rathlin just north of Rue Point. She is upright and intact. You can cover the whole wreck in one dive and there are plenty of penetration opportunities. The site teems with life and there are large schools of pollock around the bow. You will always find plenty of scallops on the seabed around the wreck too.

Rathlin North Wall: by Freda

This is an incredible dive, although maybe not for a novice diver, with the cliff wall starting at 20m and going down beyond 200m. In crystal clear water, the scenery is stunning and

resembles nothing so much as an underwater botanical garden. You also get a significant sensation of depth with the drop off falling away below you. There are two arches: one

starting at 25-35m and the second at 35-40m. You can often find crayfish nestled in the back of the arches. Jewel anemones carpet the cliff walls and orange parozoanthus hang from the arches and sway back and forth in the current.

We would usually drop in and descend to a ledge at 20m, beyond which the wall literally disappears into nothingness! The pretty kelp garden ends abruptly and becomes a sheer wall. You really need to make sure that every piece of equipment is clipped on well. I lost a reel here once, never to be seen again. The feeling is like diving over an ocean abyss. Sometimes you can get caught in eddies and it feels like being trapped in a washing machine: quite scary! Here, you can be as deep as 40m and still have razorbills and guillemots dive bombing you. They seem to like divers' bubbles and it is usually babies that come to play. They look so graceful underwater: as completely at home in the sea as they are in the air.

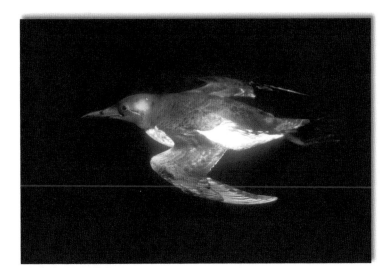

You can also see lion's mane jellyfish off the Rathlin Wall.

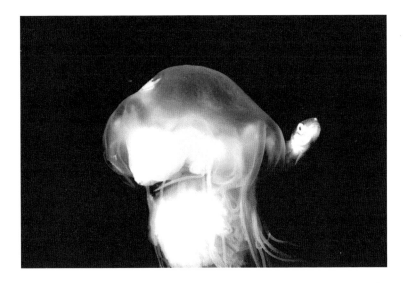

The SS Templemore: by Freda

The SS Templemore was a small coaster of 368 tons. She was carrying a cargo of coal that shifted during bad weather off Fair Head and she sank just off the entrance to Ballycastle Harbour. The wreck is fairly broken up, but the boilers are sitting upright and the propeller and shaft are still intact. This site is mainly famous for its conger eels, which are

unbelievably tame and will feed from your hands. I would often take them leftover sausages, which they enjoyed immensely. At other times I would take them some mackerel. These congers are the largest I have ever seen. They will come out of their holes and swim around you for fun, which can be a little unnerving.

I remember once diving this wreck and seeing the most unusual sight ever: a circle of as many as fifty sea hares joined to each other. Like all sea slugs, sea hares are hermaphrodite animals with fully functional male and female reproductive organs. They form mating chains, with the one at the front acting solely as a female and the one at the rear solely as a male. All the sea hares in between are acting as both males and females.

Normally, you only see a few in a row. It was truly a once-in-a-lifetime experience to see so many.

The Santa Maria: by Al

The Santa Maria is one of the most spectacular dives around Rathlin Island, albeit one of the deepest and most difficult, but it is well worth the effort and quite safe if planned properly. Because of the depth, only divers breathing a helium-based mixture should attempt it. It is particularly difficult because it lies just a mile north of Fair Head in the main tidal stream of water entering and leaving the Irish Sea. This can run at a speed of up to six knots, so it is essential to do the dive on neap tides, when slack normally arrives around 45 minutes before HW Belfast.

The Santa Maria was an American steam tanker of 5318 tons, built as the cargo ship Minnetonka in 1902 and converted into a tanker in 1906. On 25 February 1918 the German submarine UB-19 torpedoed her while she was en route to the Clyde carrying two million gallons of fuel oil. She sank, but all her crew were rescued. In the past Tommy Cecil from the Rathlin Dive Centre had a buoy on the wreck, consisting of four hard fishermen's floats spaced at different depths on the line. When slack water arrived, all four of the buoys would appear on the surface. Slack water can only last between 15 and 20 minutes, so you need to get in just as the current starts to die.

The Santa Maria lies in two halves. The bow section is the deeper half, situated at the bottom of a slope in 70m and sitting only a few metres off the seabed with the forward anchor plainly in view. The main section of the wreck lies on her starboard side in 66m, with the top of the wreck at 48m. Generally visibility is pretty good, with an average of around 15m. The accommodation section is the highest point and can be entered and explored, although with caution. Swimming further aft the stern gun can be seen lying on the seabed. Once you reach the stern, you will notice that the flagstaff is still in place and, as you swim around the jutting stern, the single huge propeller suddenly comes into view. Normally by this stage of the dive, the current has started to pick up and if you turn around you will be sheltered by the bulk of the wreck.

Once back near the shot line, it is normal practice to ascend to the highest part of the wreck, deploy your delayed SMB and jump off into the current flow. If you attempt to ascend the shot line while the current is running, you are likely to meet the four hard floats at 40m. After completing their decompression, divers usually surface near Ballycastle Bay, which is over three miles away, so good boat cover is absolutely essential.

On one memorable trip, we had a blind diver named Graham, who dived the wreck and was able to tell me there was a flagstaff still on the stern. He knew this just by touch. What an amazing guy!

10. St Kilda by Freda

St Kilda is an isolated archipelago 40 miles west-northwest of North Uist in the North Atlantic Ocean. It contains the westernmost islands of the Outer Hebrides of Scotland and I have lost count of the times we have visited this incredible Island on the Salutay. It is always a magical feeling when you arrive, because so often the weather conditions are not kind enough to get there, let alone stay.

However, the first time I went was probably my most memorable. Al invited me to join a ten-day trip in 1998, as the boat was not full and had spaces. So I jumped at the chance, managing to get time off work last minute. I was working for a car rental company at the time and had a very nice boss.

It took 36 hours to get from Port Patrick to St Kilda without stopping. I didn't expect that! Arriving at St Kilda, the weather conditions were moderate with a fresh south-easterly wind causing the Salutay to roll from side to side, which meant our anchorage for the night in Village Bay was not the most comfortable.

I remember the next morning, the sausages were cooking in the oven for breakfast, the bacon was under the grill and the eggs were on the side (on a non-slip mat) ready for frying. Al said to me "Could you keep an eye on the bacon? I'm just going to check the dive equipment is ready for the first dive." Before I knew it, I had served a full breakfast for 10 divers, which wasn't easy as a few fried eggs slid out of the pan across the cooker as Salutay took a roll. Once breakfast was over, I started to feel a little sea sick. Then it dawned on me. Where was Michael, the cook from the last trip that I was on?

I later found out he was on the Ocean Youth Trust boat that week and Al and Danny, a good friend from his Plymouth university days, were meant to be doing the cooking. Luckily, Al's Mum had prepared wholesome homemade food for the trip in advance,

which was how they operated at the time, so it was just a matter of heating prepared meals that had been frozen. Guess who ended up doing that? No such thing as a free holiday, I thought!

My first dive was on Trouser Rock at 30m up to 10m and I jumped in to visibility of 30 to 40m. Countless seals were darting around and biting my fins and the walls were just covered in a carpet of jewel anemones of every colour imaginable! There were crayfish in the crevices of the rocks and every other underwater critter you could imagine. The site is called Trouser Rock because the shape of the rock formation is exactly the same as Wallace's trousers in the Wallace and Gromit movie. First, we dived to the bottom, then went through a triangle-shaped cave hole, swam right the way up the trouser leg and basically came out at the crutch! Which is where we met all the playful seals. The dive lasted for 70 minutes and I was on a single 15-litre cylinder with a 3-litre pony of air. We dived different dive sites during our time there and somehow I ended up cooking for the rest of the trip. Luckily my seasickness improved and I enjoyed the remaining dives at St Kilda.

It was on this trip that we got the chance to dive the only wreck at St Kilda, the steam ship SS Manor in 55m. Ken the skipper at the time (an ex-navy CPO), shotted the wreck. Danny Burton was on board and Al dived with Danny as he was on a rebreather, while I dived with Danny's wife, Caroline. On the way down the shot line, I saw one of our divers coming back up the shot line with a bell under his arm and a seal (that he was completely unaware of) swimming up behind him! Was I hallucinating? Or was I already narked? No, what I saw before my eyes was real. I looked back at Caroline, whose eyes were as wide as mine. We OK'd each other, carried on down the shot and had a fantastic dive.

When Caroline and I came back to the surface, there was an altercation on board between two of our divers about whose bell it was. Ken had to break up the fight and Al said the bell had to go to the museum on the Island, which is what happened. The following night in the Puff Inn pub in Village Bay, we held a ceremony and handed the bell over to the National Trust warden for safekeeping; and to keep the peace between the two divers. We anchored for the night in Glenn Bay, which is at the opposite end of the island from Village Bay. Because the wind was in the southeast, it was more comfortable here with less rolling around at anchor.

The next morning we dived The Saw-cut. This is a narrow cut, about 1.3m wide and 25m deep, which penetrates 60m into the island of Doon. The walls are sheer and coated with anemones, soft coral and sponges. We had to make sure we didn't get swept right through the cut and come out the other side. Otherwise, Ken the skipper would be very angry, as this would make for a difficult pick up. Luckily, I was with Al and he made sure we turned around at the right point to return to where we started and get back on board safely. Then we dived Scarbhstac arch on Boreray, which was an incredible dive, as the

arch was so big and wide with currents running along the side of the cave wall. Once you came through the arch, you just finned along the magnificent wall covered in jewel anemones of every colour imaginable. Our last dive was at Boreray with caves and tunnels and endless clear blue water. It was then time to head back to the mainland. It was quite rough, so we had sandwiches along the way, but the weather improved and we had a comfortable passage back to Port Patrick, diving along the way to break up the journey.

I remember another trip back from St Kilda. It was an amazingly calm day and the divers had been on deck watching out for wild life, when I called them in for lunch. Once I served lunch to everybody, I brought Al's lunch up to the bridge. Just as Al stood up, a minke

whale leapt out of the water, breaching! It was an absolutely magnificent sight and boy did we scream! The divers came rushing out of the saloon with cameras in hand. The whale breached again and again. Rohan Holt managed to get a photo of it in the distance!

We had dinner tied up alongside at Lochmaddy Isle of North Uist. It was Fish and Chip Night. I think we can say we are the only British liveaboard to have a deep fat fryer with two large baskets. I cooked the breaded fish (or mackerel straight from the sea if we had caught some that day). The chips were deep-fried and were always to die for. We generally tried to do a scallop dive on Fish and Chip Day, so you can imagine it was always a feast, served with crushed peas and rocket.

St Kilda is famous for its Soay sheep, a breed of domestic sheep descended from a population of feral sheep. They are hardy and are particularly useful for Soay's ecosystem because they are very agile and sure-footed, which enables them to graze places that domesticated sheep cannot.

11. Sound of Mull & Coll: by Al & Freda

Oban was the pick up point for our divers to dive the Sound of Mull for long weekends and some trips to St Kilda in the later years. There was a time back in the 1990s, when the North Pier had 6 to 8 liveaboard charter boats waiting for divers on a Friday night. It was not unusual to see 80 or 90 divers on pick up night. Sadly those days have gone and now you will be lucky to find just one or two.

On our 4-day trips we always tried to get out to Coll, if the weather would allow, as there were two fabulous dives out there, the Tapti Wreck and the Yellow Brick Road. Coll is an Island west of Mull and is known for its beaches, which rise to form large sand dunes. It is also famous for its corncrakes, and for Breacachadh Castle.

The Tapti Wreck: by Freda

The Tapti was 127m long and weighed 6609 tons. She was in ballast from the Mersey to Tynemouth, when she ran aground in a storm on the southeast corner of Coll.

I first dived this wreck from the charter boat Harry Slater, which was my first experience of liveaboard diving. It was run by an amazing couple, Jan and Dave. Sadly they have both passed away now after running the liveaboard for over 25 years. The Tapti lies in 15 to 25m and is scattered. The wreck has collapsed to starboard, leaving the keel against the rocks and the deck laid out flat on the sand. The boilers have rolled out of the hull, the orientation of the fire holes showing that they are upside-down. Almost off the wreck on the starboard side, a cargo winch indicates the location of a hold between the wheelhouse and the stoke hold and engine-room.

The wreckage lies on a sandy seabed and, while most of the superstructure is covered in kelp, the main mast is spread out on the seabed and is covered in dead men's fingers. The bridge is upside down but still provides some swimthroughs. This is where we would often be greeted by a seal or two, an experience that made an already fantastic dive even better. They were always so playful, darting in and out of the bridge area.

After the seals got bored with us, we would swim towards the bow section, which is broken off. The anchor winch is immediately visible and as you swim around the bow you can see the main anchor still in place in its hawse pipe.

At this point it is a good idea to start swimming south to end your dive. If you surface too close to the rock or drift into the bay, it is difficult to pick you up.

The Yellow Brick Road: by Freda

This dive was a secret dive site that Dave from the Harry Slater would take us on. Eventually he gave Al the co-ordinates so we could take Salutay divers there. It is a scenic dive with an abundance of life. The current runs fast, which is why it is so colourful.

It is named The Yellow Brick Road, because of a feature that really looks like an underwater pathway made out of yellow sea sponges, which just goes on forever. The dive starts at 18m and slopes downwards to about 50m, where the current can be quite

strong. Sometimes there are hundreds, if not thousands, of tiny scallops called Queenies fluttering all along the yellow brick road: always an incredible sight to see.

One day, just before a dive on The Yellow Brick Road, my VR3 dive computer bounced over the side while I was kitting up. I jumped in straight after it, thinking I might be lucky enough to find it but of course I didn't. Several years later a scallop fisherman found it in his nets. It had my name and number on it and he very kindly retuned it to me. It had a few barnacles attached, but I put a new battery in and it worked perfectly.

12. Belfast Lough & the Ards Peninsula:

by Al

Belfast Lough is a sheltered sea lough on the northeast coast of Ireland. At its widest point it is six miles across and it terminates at the Port of Belfast and the mouth of the river Lagan. Its sheltered natural harbour has made it an ideal location for ship-building over the last three hundred years. Its most famous shipyard is of course Harland and Wolff, which, among others, built the great liners Titanic, Olympic and Britannic.

There are many shipwrecks in Belfast Lough, mainly losses from the First and Second World Wars. Here are a few that are regularly dived.

SS Chirripo

The Chirripo was a local ship of 4050 tons, built in 1906 by the Workman Clark shipyard. She was acquired by Elders and Fyffes as part of their fleet for the banana trade between Jamaica and Avonmouth. During WW 1 she was armed with a stern gun for defence. On 28 December 1917, while outward bound, she struck a mine laid by the German submarine UC-75 and sank half a mile southeast of Black Head Lighthouse. All the crew were rescued.

The wreck now lies in 28m on her starboard side, with the shallowest point at 16m. She is relatively intact with most of her handrails still in place. As you swim around the ship, take care that you do not get disorientated in poor visibility and swim into one of the large holds or the engine room by mistake.

In the early 1990s, access to the engine room was difficult so a friend of mine (who will remain nameless) found a hedgehog antisubmarine mortar on the wreck of the Rose nearby and carefully raised it.

He stowed it carefully in his RIB, motored over to the Chirripo and laid it on the seabed next to the engine room. Then, he contacted the Royal Navy and told them what he had "found". The Navy promptly sent some divers down to blow it up. My friend had hoped that the explosion would blow a large hole in the wreck to allow access to the engine room but unfortunately the hole the Navy guys created was too small. But it was a start and, over the years, the hole has become larger and now it is easy to get in.

Thanks to the good current flow here, the wreck is covered in soft marine growth and dead men's fingers. In good visibility, the view from the seabed of the wreck towering overhead is striking indeed.

Generally here, you have over an hour of slack water on either side of high and low water Belfast. Once the current picks up you can normally shelter in the lee of the wreck. The Chirripo is a great wreck to explore for divers of all levels and it makes a great introduction to deeper wreck diving for less experienced divers.

SS Tiberia

The Tiberia is one of the deeper wrecks in Belfast Lough and for a long time she was the benchmark for local divers embarking on deeper diving.

The 4880-ton Tiberia was built by Northumberland Shipbuilding in Newcastle in 1913 and was originally named Frimley. She was purchased and renamed by the Anchor Line in 1916. In February 1918, the U-boat UB-19 torpedoed her 1.5 miles east of Black Head as she was en route from the Clyde to New York with general cargo. She sank with no casualties.

The wreck today sits upright in 63m and the deck is at 50m. Visibility is generally good but it is dark down there. As the wreck is upright and in one piece it is quite easy to find your way around. The main accommodation is amidships and a set of lifeboat davits is clearly visible, swung out over the side to allow the ship's boat to be launched quickly. As the deckhouse was made of wood, the bridge and wheelhouse have collapsed, but there are still some interesting things to be found buried in the silt.

As you swim aft and around the engine room, where the deck drops away, you will see evidence of the damage done by the torpedo. Swimming further aft past the two holds will bring you to the poop deck, where the stern gun is situated along with a spare propeller. The gun is one of the highlights of the shipwreck and points menacingly out over the side, covered in soft sponges and dead men's fingers. On both the poop deck and forecastle, access ladders are still in place. The forward mast has collapsed.

Good boat cover is essential for this dive, as the Tiberia lies on the main shipping route into Belfast Lough. While you are decompressing, you will clearly hear ships passing close by.

SS Neotsfield

Beyond the sheltered waters of Belfast Lough and out in the Irish Sea lies the collier SS Neotsfield, sunk 1.5 miles south of the Skulmartin safe water mark.

The Neotsfield was built in 1906 by Furness Withy and Co. in West Hartlepool and weighed 3821 tons. On 14 September 1918, she was sunk by the UB-64 while en route from Glasgow to Naples carrying coal and coke. There were no casualties.

The Neotsfield lies in 48m and rises 11m above the seabed. She is upright and intact, apart from a large hole near the engine room where the torpedo struck. The bridge and accommodation are the shallowest parts of the wreck at around 36m, and they offer opportunities for safe penetration. The captain's washroom is clearly visible just below the bridge.

Swimming aft past the coal-filled holds brings you to the poop deck, where a massive 4-inch gun is situated with its barrel pointing towards the seabed. At one stage, the gun was intact and upright but over time the decking has collapsed and the gun has fallen over.

Visibility varies a lot on this wreck but you can expect 6 or 7m. For the best results, dive about 45 minutes before high water Belfast, which on small tides should give you up to one hour of slack water.

SS Hunsdon

The 2899-ton Hunsdon was originally a German vessel built by Wesser Company Bremen and named the Arnfried. She was captured by the British at Dula, West Africa on 14 July 1914, renamed and registered under a British flag.

While en route from Le Havre to Belfast, she was torpedoed by UB-92 on 18 October 1918 one mile east of Strangford Fairway buoy. There was one casualty.

The wreck of the Hunsdon is one of my favourites and, as a teenager, I learned my craft diving her several times a week from the MV Ocean Vaux run by my father. It was a popular wreck for the local dive clubs that chartered us regularly.

The Hunsdon lies in 38m and, at her shallowest point, rises to 33m on the bow and main engine. It can be a dark wreck, but visibility is generally around 3 to 6m. She lies on a sandy, gravelly seabed, which is covered with an abundance of scallops.

The wreck is well broken up with hull plating scattered over the seabed, but the main section consisting of the bridge, engine and boiler are fairly intact, as are both the forward and aft main masts, which are lying across the wreckage. If you swim back past the aft mast, you will come across the stern section, which lies on its side with a six-pounder gun pointing towards the seabed.

Slack water on this wreck is good and lasts an hour before and after high and low water Belfast.

13. SV Majorka off Cape Wrath: by Al

It was the last week of August 1997, the MV Salutay was operating out of Oban in the Firth of Lorne and we were preparing to embark on a 14-day trip to the Shetland Islands, organised as part of the BSAC expedition scheme.

The expedition was organised by Clare Peddie and she had put together an experienced group of divers who had previously dived with us in places like Malin Head and St Kilda.

The plan was to transit to Kinlochbervie, diving along the way, then make a 24-hour crossing from Cape Wrath to the Shetland Islands.

We left Oban early in the morning and went to dive an offshore pinnacle called Bo Faskadale, north of Ardnamurchan Point. Then we headed towards the Sound of Sleat, inshore of the Isle of Skye, and spent the night alongside at Kyle of Loch Alsh. The next day we transited north and dived a drop-off north of the Isle of Raasay, then made for the harbour of Kinlochbervie situated in Loch Inchard.

That evening, we discussed the possibility of diving the wreck of a sailing ship called the Majorka, northwest of Cape Wrath. She was a Norwegian three masted, fully rigged sailing ship that struck a mine laid by the German submarine U-71 in 1917. She lay in 54m, at the limit of the diving range for air, but we had an experienced group of divers on board and we expected that visibility would be good, so it would be a viable dive.

We located the site based on a position we got from a local fisherman and the image on our echo sounder showed the Majorka to be well broken up and sitting just a few metres off the seabed.

I dived first and checked the location of the shot, to make sure it was in the right place. The first pair of divers was to descend 10 minutes after me.

As I descended, I could see the Majorka stretched out below me. The offshore visibility was exceptionally good on this particular morning. I could see that the shot had landed around 10m back from the bow and was securely in place, so I decided not to bother checking it and dropped off the line to swim towards the bow section. That turned out to be a big mistake!

The first pair of divers descended onto the scattered wreckage. One of them, Bruce Humby, let go of the shot line and landed right on the bell, no more than 2m away from the shot weight. He never moved from that spot the whole dive. He dragged it free and sent it to the surface with a lift bag. What a great find!

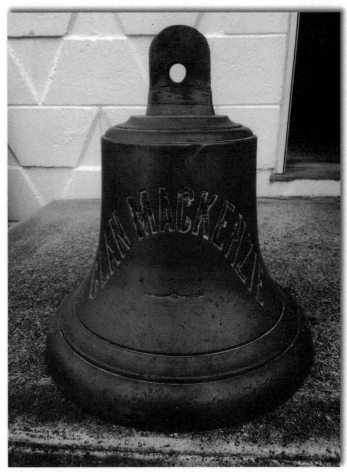

For the remainder of my bottom time, I swam around the Majorka and out across several of the masts, looking for artefacts. Unknown to me, the main prize, the soul of the ship, had already been recovered. If only I had checked the shot more closely!

After the dive had finished and everyone was safely back on board, we started work on cleaning the bell and trying to decipher the inscription we could see on it. After some careful cleaning by Bruce the name "Clan Mackenzie" became visible. We later found out that this was her original name. She had been built in Glasgow in 1882 and sold to Norway in 1909.

So, after that successful dive, we set sail on a 24-hour steam to the west side of the Shetland Islands for a week of exploration and very scenic diving.

14. Normandy D-Day Wrecks: by Freda

In 2014 we left Ireland and sailed Salutay to Poole for new adventures in France and Channel Islands.

On these charters, we usually leave in the early hours of Sunday morning and head across the Channel to Cherbourg, having breakfast along the way. Even if it isn't so calm, at least some of the divers participate. We have lunch when we get to Cherbourg before the first dive or after the second dive depending on the tide and slack water. We generally tie up in Cherbourg in the marina to get a good night's sleep, before heading to the Baie de Seine the next morning.

After so many years of incredible diving in Ireland, when we first came down here, I imagined I would dive less during our charters. I thought the visibility would not be as good as I was used to and that the wrecks would probably not be up to much. Well, how wrong I was!

There is no crystal clear blue water, but nevertheless, visibility is pretty good at times, in fact anything from 5 to 15m. And that, teamed with entirely intact wrecks in shallow waters with seemingly endless marine life, makes for diving that I can't get enough of.

These days we have a new Baie de Seine Big Three to rival our former Malin Head Big Three.

The Susan B. Anthony

During the time we have been running charters to Normandy and diving the D-Day wrecks, the Susan B Anthony has become my favourite dive. She was named after one of the driving forces in the women's suffrage movement. The Suzie lies in just 30m, is almost intact, and diving her is like diving in an aquarium. I have never seen so much marine life in one dive: it is just incredible!

She began life in March 1930 as a passenger steamer called the SS Santa Clara. She was acquired by the Navy on 7 August 1942 and renamed before being converted into a troopship and commissioned a month later. In June 1944, while cruising off Normandy during the D-Day landings, she struck a mine, which exploded under her number 4 hold. She immediately lost all power and listed to starboard. Efforts to tow her to shallower

water were abandoned when fire broke out in the engine and boiler rooms. The troops were evacuated to two destroyers alongside, and the crew joined them just before the Susan B. Anthony finally sank. No one was killed and few of the 45 wounded were seriously hurt.

Al and I had our best dive on her in 2016. It is rare that we can dive together but, on this occasion, we had another skipper on board, Mike Rowley. It was a warm, sunny day with a northerly wind blowing and the visibility was stunning, at least 15m. Al placed the shot at the bow section, which is still in excellent condition with teak decking and portholes. The 40mm Bofors deck gun on the bow makes a great image.

Another 3-inch gun is hidden underneath the amidships section and we were looking around there when a dolphin swam past. I immediately grabbed Al, who hadn't seen it. Then it came by again and this time he grabbed me. Neither of us could believe it. We were really excited. I had never before seen a dolphin on the wreck itself, only on the surface.

We spent 48-minutes on the wreck, then I had to get back up and put lunch on for the hungry divers. I had a little deco to do but, as we hit the surface, two dolphins started jumping in front of us. Wow, what a dive that was!

LST 523 Landing Ship Tank

The 100m-long LST 523 was built in Indianapolis in February 1944 as the USS Carbonelle to take part in Operation Overlord, the allied invasion of Europe. LSTs were larger than infantry landing craft and operated by beaching themselves. The bow doors would open,

allowing the cargo of tanks, armoured cars, bulldozers or lorries to drive off, and the LST would then wait for the flood tide to float itself off again.

Displacing 1635 tons and capable of 11 knots, LST 523 made several trips across the Channel, carrying Sherman tanks to reinforce the British forces. She finally hit a German mine on the morning of 19 June while fully loaded and, heavily damaged in the bows, turned over and sank in just two minutes, in waters 29m deep.

Al would normally shot the wreck just forward of the engine room, which gives divers a good swimthrough, especially those that get in first and get the best visibility. Inside the engine room there are always huge shoals of vivid dark blue bass swimming up, down and

around. The wreck sits upside down and the propeller shafts stand proud although, unfortunately, the propellers have been removed. The stern is brightly covered in white plumose anemones. If you swim over the top, back towards the bow, you will find upside-down Sherman tanks on the seabed just off the bow. Lobsters walk around as if they own the place and shoals of sea bream come and go.

SS Empire Broadsword

This is an outstanding dive, especially when you get great visibility, which we have been lucky enough to get most of the time. She stands an impressive 15m off the seabed and lies on her starboard side.

On 2 July 1944, almost a month after D-Day, the Broadsword was back at Omaha beach, landing troops and equipment, when she struck 2 mines. The explosions lifted the ship and broke her back. She settled on the seabed very quickly in only 25m. This means divers can spend a long time on the wreck. Mind you, I could easily spend a whole week on her and still only just see everything.

The Broadsword lies on an east/west axis. On her starboard side, she is broken just aft of the engine room and you can swim inside, although great care must be taken as many years of strong tides, gales and shallow depth have weakened the structure. When you swim from stern to bow there is so much to see. First, a massive rudder but there is no propeller, as this has been salvaged. The large 4" deck gun stand at the stern is an impressive sight, the barrel pointing skywards as if ready to fire, with lots of ammunition

scattered around. Passing the engine room, you come to the bridge area, still large and pretty intact, giving great penetration access, but you can or should only go inside when there is good visibility. On the fore deck there are more guns, both 4-inch and smaller anti-aircraft guns as well as more munitions. The toilet block is magnificent to see, with sinks and taps still attached, hanging upside down from the floor, which is now the ceiling. Toilets lie scattered around. Large scallops can be found around the edges of the wreckage. This is a fantastic dive. You could dive it every day for a week and you would still want to come back for more.

15. The Leopoldville: by Al

The SS Leopoldville is one of the most impressive wrecks in the English Channel, as well as one of the most tragic, due to the needless loss of over 800 American troops. She was built in 1929 as a passenger liner and operated between Antwerpen and the Belgian Congo. During the war she was requisitioned to serve as a troop transport between Southampton and Cherbourg.

On Christmas Eve 1944, she was anchored five miles north of Cherbourg with over 2235 American troops on board, when she was torpedoed by the U-486. Distress signals by radio were slow to be answered, due to the Christmas celebrations ashore. Eventually, the British destroyer HMS Brilliant came alongside the listing vessel, which was not an easy task, and took as many troops off as she could safely hold. The remainder of the troops perished, as they had not been taught how to launch the ship's lifeboats. The Belgian crew had already abandoned ship, leaving the Americans to their fate.

The wreck today lies on her port side in 55m. Her highest point is at 38m. She is almost fully intact apart from the stern, which has broken off. As you swim along the top rail, you can see lifeboat davits as well as a lot of fishing line left by local anglers.

Of all the shipwrecks I have dived, the Leopoldville is probably the spookiest, mainly because of how she towers over you and the fact that, as you swim through the companionways and superstructure, evidence of the lost American soldiers lies all around you. Boots, gasmasks, helmets and rifles can all be seen sticking out of the silt. These artefacts lend perspective to the tragic loss of life that took place on this vessel and, as a mark of respect, nothing should be touched or taken. The Leopoldville is a designated war grave and a permit must be obtained from the French authorities to visit her. Most divers find her a sobering and thought-provoking ship to dive on.

16. Kayaking the Channel Isles: by Al

We have run a number of kayak trips from the MV Salutay around the Channel Isles and many of the outlying reefs around these tide-swept islands. Our first stopping off point after an overnight steam is usually Alderney.

Alderney

Alderney is known as the "rock in the river" in kayaking speak, due to the strong currents that flow around it. Advanced tidal planning is essential and we normally kayak this island on a neap tide, which gives paddlers some latitude in timing and makes it a more relaxing paddle.

Our starting point is Braye Harbour. We normally then paddle anti-clockwise, to catch the last of the south going tidal stream down the Swinge Channel between Alderney and Burhou. Usually, we stay close in against the rock to avoid any overfalls, which can be quite dramatic and frightening, if there is any wind against the tide.

A ferry glide is normally required to paddle across to a group of rocks on the southwest corner called Les Etacs, which are home for the largest population of nesting gannets in the English Channel. Once you have come around the southern tip of Alderney and are clear of the worst of the Swinge overfalls and currents, you can relax as you go along the east coast of the island. A ruined pier to the southeast, which, in the past, allowed ships to load and unload cargo, is an interesting stopping point, as are Raz Island and Longy Bay.

As you approach the northern tip of the island, the tidal streams increase, but if you get the timing right, they will sweep you around the northern point and past the Mannez lighthouse. If not, then close rock-hopping is required to stay in the eddies and avoid the worst of the current. The northern tip of Alderney is quite spectacular and, as you paddle back into Braye Harbour, you can see remnants of the German occupation in the form of pillbox machine gun posts and bunkers.

Herm Island

Herm Island lies approximately 3 nautical miles east of St Peter Port in Guernsey. It is only 1.5 miles long and half a mile wide and, as it so small, cars and bicycles are banned.

Tidal streams here are not as critical as at Alderney but it is still a good idea to have favourable flow in the direction you want to travel. So, again we normally paddle this island anti-clockwise starting at Jethou, which is a small island on the southeast corner, then heading towards the northern tip of Herm, which has beautiful sandy beaches that are ideal for a stop and some snorkelling. Then, paddling past Oyster Point and south towards the harbour is very pleasant, and a stop at the harbour for an ice cream is highly recommended.

Sark

Sark involves a full day of paddling and the Salutay normally anchors in the bay at La Grande Greve, when the weather allows. Depending on the tides, the island can be circumnavigated via either the north or south.

An interesting rock hop and circumnavigation is the island of Brecqhou, just to the northwest of our anchorage. Unfortunately this island is privately owned and landing is strictly forbidden, but the castle is rather interesting architecturally, with its towers, buttresses and helicopter pad.

The southern tip of Sark has higher ground and cliffs, but there are two safe landing bays in the southeast that are often used as anchorages by visiting yachts. Creux Harbour, on the eastern side, is Sark's main harbour and there is a tunnel cut through the rocks that leads to the rest of the island. Depending on the tidal stream, on either side of the harbour there are sometimes small overfalls, which can be entertaining.

Overfalls can also be encountered at the northern tip of Sark, around the rocks of Bec du Nez, and these can give you a fun few minutes until they spit you out into calmer waters.

All in all, Sark is a great place to paddle, with a bit of everything for the sea kayaker, from sheltered sandy bays to playful tide races on the headlands.

Recipes from the Salutay Galley

Chef

Snacks from the Galley

Raw Cashew, Almond & Cranberry Flapjacks

Serves 12 - 2 small squares each

Ingredients

150g cashew nuts
150g ground almonds
90g dried cranberries
70g coconut oil (slightly melted in microwave)
Pinch of Himalayan pink salt
One level dessertspoon of set honey

Method

Whiz the cashew nuts up in a food processor for a couple of minutes.
Add the ground almonds and salt and whiz for another minute or two.
Add the cranberries, melted coconut oil, honey and whiz everything together until the mixture forms a lump and is fully mixed up.
Tip out into a 24 x 16 cm tray (a little smaller is fine too) lined with cling film and press the mixture down flat using a palate knife. Pop into the freezer for about 5 minutes until the mixture is hard, but pliable enough to cut.
Carefully place onto a chopping board, whip away the cling film and cut into 24 squares.
Must be kept in the fridge in an airtight container. Will keep for up to 2 weeks.
These are super delicious and Al's favourite and a very healthy alternative to my cakes.
They are gluten & dairy free and suitable for vegans if you use an alternative to honey.

Top Tip

These flapjacks freeze really well so you can take a few out at a time when you want them.

Raw Chocolate, Date & Pecan Brownies

Serves 12 - 2 small squares each

Ingredients

150g pecan nuts
150g dates (stones removed)
50g cacao powder
50g coconut oil (slightly melted in the microwave)
Pinch of Himalayan pink salt
One flat dessertspoon of set honey
One dessertspoon of any peanut butter

Method

Whiz the pecan nuts up first in a food processor for a couple of minutes.
Add the dates and salt and whiz for another 2 to 3 minutes.
Add the honey, peanut butter, melted coconut oil and cacao and whiz everything together until the mixture forms a lump and is fully mixed up.
Tip out into a 24cm x 16cm tray (a little smaller is fine too), lined with cling film, and press the mixture down flat using a palate knife. Pop into the freezer for about 5 minutes until the mixture is hard, but pliable enough to cut.
Carefully place onto a chopping board, whip away the cling film and cut into 24 squares.
Must be kept in the fridge in an airtight container. Will keep for up to 2 weeks.
These are my favourite and stop me from eating a whole season of cakes. They are both gluten-free and dairy-free and suitable for vegans if you use an alternative to honey.

Top Tip

These also freeze really well so you can take a few out at a time when you want them.

Sweet Spiced Cupcakes

Serves 12 – I cupcake each

Ingredients

180g self-raising flour
180g butter
90g castor sugar
90g dark brown soft sugar
3 large eggs
1 heaped tsp baking powder
One third of a jar of good quality mincemeat
A large hand full Omega 3 mix seeds (sunflower, pumpkin, linseeds)
Icing sugar to dust

Method

Place all the ingredients - except for the mincemeat and seed mix - in one large bowl and mix with an electric mixer until light and very fluffy.
Add the mincemeat and mix again for a minute or two.
Divide the mixture between 12 cupcake cases in a large 12-cupcake tin.
Bang the tray on a bench to release any air trapped in the cupcakes.
Sprinkle the seed mix over the top of each cake.
Cook them in a pre-heated oven at 180°C, gas mark 4, for 25 to 30 minutes.
Use a cake tester (thin skewer) to check that they are done (or eat one).
Enjoy, either straight from the oven with a blob of clotted cream or many days later.

Top Tip

Again, these cupcakes also freeze really well.

Banana & Almond Cupcakes

Makes 12 large cupcakes

Ingredients

180g self-raising flour
180g butter
90g castor sugar
90g dark brown soft sugar
3 large eggs
1 heaped tsp baking powder
2 small/medium ripe bananas
A handful of flaked almonds
Icing sugar to dust before serving (optional)

Method

Mix all the ingredients, except for the bananas and the almonds, with an electric mixer in a large bowl for about 5 minutes non-stop, until everything is light and very fluffy. Don't forget to scrape the bowl down using a spatula.
Divide the mixture between 12 cupcake cases in a large 12-cupcake tin.
Cut the bananas into chunks and put about 3 chunks into each cupcake.
Sprinkle almonds on top of each one.
Bang the tray on a bench to release any air trapped in the cupcakes.
Place them in a pre-heated oven at 180°C, gas mark 4, for 25 to 30 minutes. Use a cake tester (thin skewer) to check that they are done (or eat one).
These cakes turn out amazing every time and last for quite a few days, (that is, if they are around for that long). They also freeze really well. For gluten-free cakes, replace the flour with gluten-free flour. For dairy-free cakes, just use a non-dairy alternative.

Top Tip

Over -ripe bananas make the centre an oozy delight.

Chocolate Biscuit Cake

Serves 12 large portions or 24 normal portions.

Ingredients

400g digestive biscuits
400g 55% dark chocolate
200g milk chocolate
4.5 tbsp golden syrup
200g butter
Decoration (optional)
100g white chocolate
Small handful mini marshmallows
100s and 1,000s or freeze-dried raspberries or crumbed nuts as you wish

Method

Place the butter, golden syrup and chocolate broken into pieces in a large microwavable bowl and melt for about 2 minutes on high. Then take it out and stir for another minute or two if needed. It melts very quickly. Stir until you get a rich, velvety consistency.
Break the biscuits and add them to the mixture. Stir thoroughly until the chocolate coats all the biscuits. Using a spatula, scrape the mixture into a 33 x 18 cm tin lined with NON-STICK silver foil.
Melt the white chocolate in the microwave and pour it over the cake in up and down directions, then use a knife to drag the chocolate around to make a swirly pattern.
Finish off with freeze-dried raspberry pieces or your choice of decoration and refrigerate for at least an hour. Then take it out of the fridge and bring it back to almost room temperature before cutting it into 12 slabs.
I usually cut the slabs in two again to make 24 portions, as they are very rich.
We usually have these after a dive on the Leopoldville, before we set off back to Portland. They last for a few days, freeze really well and take no time to defrost. Leftovers taste fabulous with a cuppa out on deck after a dive.

Top Tip

If you don't have a microwave you can melt the chocolate mixture in a saucepan. It works just as well.

Coffee and Walnut Cupcakes

Makes 12 large cupcakes

Ingredients

180g self-raising flour
180g butter
90g castor sugar
90g dark brown soft sugar
3 large eggs
1 heaped tsp baking powder
1 tbsp of coffee essence or thick Instant coffee
12 halved walnuts to decorate
Cocoa powder

For the icing
180g icing sugar
180g softened butter
1 tbsp of coffee essence or thick instant coffee

Method

Using an electric mixer, mix all the ingredients, except for the walnuts and coffee essence, in a large bowl for about 5 minutes non-stop, until the mixture is light and very fluffy.
Add the coffee essence and mix for another minute or two.
Divide the mixture between 12 cupcake cases in a large 12-cupcake tin.
Bang the tray on a bench to release any air trapped in the cupcakes.
Place them in a pre-heated oven at 180°C, gas mark 4, for 25 to 30 minutes. Use a cake tester (thin skewer) to check that they are done (or eat one).
Mix the icing ingredients thoroughly, using an electric whisk, until it is soft and creamy.
Divide the mixture between the 12 cupcakes. Spread it evenly or pipe it over each cake.
Pop half a walnut on top to finish. Dust with cocoa powder.
I love these, but sadly I only make them on the occasional trip because there are just not enough days in the week.

Top Tip

A thick espresso makes these cakes taste just divine!

Green Tea Cake

Serves 12

Ingredients

240g sultanas
240ml of strong green tea
180g self-raising flour
90g dark brown sugar
1 heaped tsp of baking powder
1 large egg

Method

Soak the sultanas in the green tea for 4 hours in a large bowl with a lid, stirring occasionally.
Add the rest of the ingredients to the soaked fruit and stir with a wooden spoon until thoroughly mixed.
Tip the mixture into a 1lb lined loaf tin and bake in a reheated oven at 180°C, gas mark 4 for 40-45 minutes. Check to see if it's cooked by using a cake tester.
It should come out as clean as a ships whistle. Leave in the tin for 5 minutes or so and then take out and rest on a wire rack leaving it in the paper liner.
This cake slices beautifully and is even more delicious when buttered lavishly.

Top Tip

If green tea really isn't your thing, then try Earl Grey or just normal every day tea instead.

Lavender Shortbread Fish

Makes 12 fish plus extra for testing

Ingredients

120g soft butter
60g castor sugar
Extra sugar for sprinkling
100g plain flour
80g corn flour
Extra flour for rolling
Edible food grade lavender (optional)

Method

Using an electric mixer, whisk the butter and sugar together until smooth. Add the flour and corn flour and continue to whisk until almost combined.

Turn it out onto a floured work surface and gently roll it out until the paste is about 1cm thick, (NO LESS). Sprinkle the lavender over it and lightly roll it again to press in. Use a cutter to cut out the fish, dipping the cutter into the flour each time before cutting. Place them onto a non-stick baking tray. You should easily get 12 fish. Sprinkle them with a little sugar and chill them in the fridge for 30 minutes to firm them up.

Heat the oven to 170°C, gas mark 3.

Bake in the oven for 20 minutes or until it just starts to crisp around the tail edges. Then, take them out and, using a palate knife, carefully lift the fish onto a wire rack to cool. You can cut the leftover bits of shortbread pastry into shapes and bake them too. Eat them straight from the oven as your testers. Don't keep re-rolling shortbread, as it will just fall apart.

Store in an airtight container. The fish freeze well and are quick to defrost.

Top Tip

Non-stick silver foil is amazing stuff, especially when your baking trays are no longer as non-stick as they used to be.

Flapjacks

Makes 12

Ingredients

240g butter
200g Demerara sugar
2 level tbsp golden syrup
420g rolled porridge oats (in a large container)
50g Omega mix seeds

Method

Melt the butter, sugar and golden syrup in a saucepan and bring to the boil until all is dissolved. Remove the liquid from the heat, pour it over the oats and mix well. Then, tip the mixture into a 28 x 18 x 3 cm baking tray lined with non-stick silver foil. Smooth down roughly and then sprinkle the Omega mix seeds evenly over the top. Press the seeds down flat using the back of a spoon.
Cook it in the centre of the oven at 180°C, gas mark 4, for 30 to 40 minutes. Check it after 30 minutes. If it is golden around the edges then it is done. Leave it to cool down in the tin, covered with a tea towel.
Once it has cooled, take it out of the tin, carefully peel off the silver foil and cut it into 12 pieces or 24 triangles. Store in an airtight container.

Top Tip

You can add almost anything to these flapjacks. Try 3 level tsp of chopped ginger in syrup with pecan nuts or you could just leave them plain and spread melted chocolate over the top. Again, these freeze really well.

Triple Chocolate Cupcakes

Makes 12 large cupcakes

Ingredients

150g self-raising flour
30g cocoa powder
180g butter
180g dark brown soft sugar
3 large eggs
1 heaped tsp baking powder
1 tbsp milk
120g mixture of white, dark and milk chocolate pieces (suitable for baking)

Method

Put all the ingredients, except for the chocolate pieces, in one large bowl and mix with an electric mixer until light and very fluffy. This will take about 5 minutes non-stop.
Divide the mixture between 12 cupcake cases in a large 12-cupcake tin.
Bang the tray on a bench to release any air trapped in the cupcakes.
Carefully place equal quantities of the chocolate pieces on top of each cake, pushing them into the mixture. Place them into a pre-heated oven at 180°C, gas mark 4, for 25 to 30 minutes. Use a cake tester (thin skewer) to check that they are done (or eat one).

Top Tip

Instead of adding chocolate pieces to the mixture I sometimes bake them plain and once they have cooled down I top them with chocolate spread and put a seashell chocolate on top. As you can imagine, these get a pretty good reception. In the unlikely event that any are left over, they freeze well.

Al and Freda diving TOGETHER!

Soups from the Galley

Lentil, Butterbean and Spinach Soup

Serves 4

Ingredients

1 tbsp olive oil or coconut oil
1 large white onion & I medium red onion, both chopped
240g red split lentils
1 litre vegetable stock
Salt and pepper
Half a finely sliced red pepper or a large tomato on the vine, (or both)
Frozen spinach (you can use fresh), up to you how much you put in.
400g tinned butter beans, drained
A good squeeze of lemon or lime juice

Method

Heat the oil and sweat the white onion, add the lentils and keep stirring until they are all coated with oil and onions. Add a good grind of salt and pepper. Pour in the stock, stir and add the frozen spinach, red onion and red pepper/tomato. Let simmer for a good 20 minutes until the lentils have gone soft. Then add the drained butterbeans. Leave to rest for several hours before re-heating and eating.
Garnish with sprouted alfalfa, red clover or mung beans, (see the section on Sprouting at Sea), along with flat leaf parsley and fresh thyme if you wish, then add a squeeze of lemon or lime just before you serve. This soup is a favourite on board MV Salutay. We have it on a Sunday during the crossing to Cherbourg, before or after the first dive (depending on the tides). I make it after breakfast so it can sit for several hours, giving it time to reach a rich depth of flavour and texture.

Top Tip

This soup is even more delicious if you add a spoonful of curry powder when you put the lentils in. To make this soup for 12, just use three times the ingredients and freeze it into portions.

Carrot, Coriander and Ginger Soup

Serves 4

Ingredients

2 tbsp olive oil
30g butter
1 large white onion chopped
6 carrots peeled and roughly chopped
200g left over champ or 200g raw potatoes peeled and chopped
1 litre vegetable stock
½ tsp dried ginger & 2 level tsp dried coriander
Salt and pepper
70g fresh coriander

Method

Heat the oil and sweat the onion, add the carrot and sauté gently until slightly soft.
Add a good grind of salt and pepper, the dried ginger and dried coriander and mix thoroughly.
Add the boiling stock and simmer for 30 to 40 minutes, then put the champ in and simmer gently for another 30 to 40 minutes. If you are using raw potatoes, then put them in with the carrots. (I use champ because I make extra champ on Chicken and Haggis Night and keep it for my soups).
Just before serving, liquidize the soup to a smooth consistency and then add the chopped fresh coriander. Remember to hold some back for the garnish.
Garnish with sprouted alfalfa, red clover or mung beans.
This soup is delicious and extra special if you add ginger, which can help prevent or assist your recovery from seasickness. (Even if it doesn't work, at least it will taste better when it comes back up!)
I make the soup after breakfast, so it can sit for several hours giving it time to reach a rich depth of flavour and texture.

Top Tip

Add ginger to everything if you are at sea and struggling with seasickness. They do say even rubbing raw ginger on your wrists can help. To make this soup for 12, just use three times the ingredients and freeze it into portions.

Yellow Split Pea and Courgette Soup

Serves 4

Ingredients

2 tbsp olive oil
2 onions finely chopped
300g yellow split peas
3 grated courgettes
1.5 litres chicken or vegetable stock
1 level tsp turmeric
Sea salt and pepper
4 dollops of natural yogurt
Fresh mint leaves (Optional)

Method

Place the yellow split peas in a bowl, cover them with cold water and leave them to soak over night. Drain them, rinse them and drain them again.

Heat the oil in a large saucepan. Add the onions, stirring occasionally until soft and slightly caramelized. Then, add the stock, split peas, turmeric, salt and pepper and bring to the boil.

When the peas are softened, liquidize them and then add the grated courgettes. Continue to cook until the courgettes are just cooked.

Serve with a dollop of thick natural yogurt and a sprinkling of mint and cracked black pepper.

I don't make this soup very often these days, but it was always a favourite on our 10-day trips to St Kilda and Malin Head.

Top Tip

To make this soup for 12, just use three times the ingredients and freeze it into portions.

Vegetable or Vegetable & Chicken Soup

Serves 4

Ingredients

2 tbsp olive oil
1 large white onion chopped
Any leftover vegetables you want to use up.
1 bag of frozen casserole mixed vegetables
200g leftover champ or 200g raw potatoes peeled and chopped.
750ml vegetable stock
Salt and pepper

Method

Heat the oil and sweat the onion, add any leftover raw vegetables and sauté everything gently until it is slightly soft. Add the frozen casserole mix and a good grind of salt and pepper. Continue to cook for another 15 minutes or so.
Add the boiling stock and simmer for about 45 minutes, then add the champ and simmer gently for another 30 minutes. If you are using raw potatoes then add them at the raw vegetable stage.
Just before serving, liquidize the soup until it is smooth.
Garnish with sprouted alfalfa, red clover, mung beans or freshly sliced spinach. (See the section on Sprouting at Sea)
Again, I make this after breakfast so it can sit for several hours, giving it time to reach a rich depth of flavour and texture.

Top Tip

I adapt this soup recipe quite a bit depending on whether I have vegetarians, vegans or people with dairy intolerances on board. If there are no vegetarians, I use leftover chicken stock and cooked chicken pieces that I have left over from the chicken and haggis dish. This makes the soup really hearty. Also, crème fraiche makes the soup lovely and creamy.

Al & Ed paddle-boarding next to Salutay in Poole Harbour

Main Courses from the Galley

Cross Channel Curry

Serves 4

Ingredients

12 chicken thighs (skin removed)
2 tbsp olive oil
2 tsp cumin seeds and 1 fresh green chili, sliced thinly (leave out the chili for a mild curry)
1tsp freshly minced garlic
1tsp freshly minced ginger
I large white onion, sliced
1 red onion, sliced
12 cherry tomatoes sliced in half
2 tsp cumin powder
2 tsp turmeric
1 tsp chili powder (½ tsp for a mild curry)
2 tsp coriander powder
1 tsp garam masala (Naina & Raj style)(see page 154) (½ tsp for a mild curry)
1 red pointed pepper sliced
2 tbsp mango chutney:
200ml chicken stock
Pinch of salt
120ml crème fraiche or coconut milk
Fresh coriander leaves (optional)

Method

Place the chicken thighs on a baking tray, season with salt and pepper and roast in the oven for 45 to 50 minutes at 180°C, gas mark 4, turning them several times until cooked and golden brown.
Heat the oil in a deep pan, fry the cumin seeds for a couple of minutes and then add the chili, garlic, ginger and fry gently. Add the onions, peppers, tomatoes and the rest of the dry spices and cook gently. Add the chicken stock, mango chutney, salt and finally the crème fraiche or coconut milk and simmer slowly.
When the chicken is cooked, add it to the curry sauce. If you think your curry sauce is too thick, add the chicken juices to thin it. Sprinkle with fresh coriander leaves just before serving.
I usually serve this curry for dinner while we are halfway across the Channel, so it needs to be simple, and I make it earlier in the afternoon to give it some time to mature. I remember one very rough journey after diving the Leopoldville. It was getting dark, and the divers were getting hungry. I was trying to serve the curry and I lost two of my lovely black Colombian dishes, when they fell and were smashed to pieces. We decided to postpone dinner until we got back to Portland to enjoy the curry in calmer waters. I now use metal serving dishes!

Top Tip

Make the sauce in advance and add the crème fraiche when you reheat it, unless you are using coconut milk.

Pork Loin Steak Stack with Onion and Chorizo Stuffing

Serves 2

Ingredients

4 pork loin steaks
Sea salt and pepper

Stuffing
15g butter
1 tbsp olive oil
1 chopped onion
1 tbsp finely sliced kale
1 egg
1 large slice of bread made into breadcrumbs
Sea salt and pepper
4 ready-sliced chorizo pieces cut into thin strips

Method

For the stuffing, heat the oil and butter in a heavy pan, add the onion and chorizo and sauté gently for a few minutes, then add the kale and continue to cook until just soft.
Take off the heat and allow to cool before adding the breadcrumbs, seasoning and egg.
Bind together adding a little water if necessary.
Tip the mix into a small, greased non-stick oven dish and bake it for about 25 minutes in a pre-heated oven at 180°C, gas mark 4.
After 15 minutes cover it lightly with silver foil.
Lay the pork loin steaks on a large flat baking tray suitable for grilling, season with salt and pepper and leave at room temperature for 20 minutes before cooking.
Grill for 15 to 18 minutes on medium to high until the crackling is golden and crispy. Turn them over half way through cooking.
Place one steak on the plate and put a spoonful of the stuffing mixture on top followed by the second steak to create a stack. Hold them in place with a flagged cocktail stick.
Serve with ratatouille (see page 122), sweet corn and roast potatoes in their skins.

Top Tip

If you have a griddle pan, use this to cook the pork. You can also double or triple the quantities to make extra stuffing that can be frozen for next time.

"Chillox" Chilli Con Carne

Makes 12 large portions

Ingredients

5 tbsp olive oil
5 x 500g good quality lean steak mince
5 large onions, chopped
5 garlic cloves, crushed
2½ tbsp chili powder
2½ tbsp paprika
2½ tbsp cumin powder
2½ tbsp tomato puree
2½ tbsp plain flour (or gluten-free flour)
Pinch of sea salt
3 tins of chopped tomatoes 400g
2 tins kidney beans 400g (drained)
2 green peppers, chopped into chunks

Method

Heat the oil and add the onion and mincemeat. Once the meat starts to cook, add the garlic, stirring constantly to break up the meat (Al's job).
Once the meat is cooked and the juices are bubbling, add the chilli powder, paprika, cumin, tomato puree, plain flour and salt, mixing quickly and thoroughly.
Cook for a further 10 minutes-ish until all the ingredients are well mixed in.
Add the tomatoes, peppers and kidney beans and mix it thoroughly, while gently bringing it to the boil.
Then lower the heat and cover and simmer for about 45 minutes, stirring to prevent the meat from sticking.
Turn the heat off, but leave the lid on. When you are ready to serve, reheat it all the way through until it is piping hot.
I normally cook "Chillox" after lunch, so it has time to reach a rich depth of flavour by dinnertime. Serve with rice, tortillas, grated cheese, sour cream and Death By Sauce for those who like it REALLY HOT.
Nowadays our chilli is cooked on board, but in the old days I used to make it pre-season and freeze it. It was Danny Burton who came up with the name after a long Easter weekend of rebreather training, when the only food he and Al had to eat was a 12-person batch of chilli. After 4 days, the atmosphere inside the cabin was no longer air, it could only be described as mixed gas – hence "Chillox" was born.

Top Tip

If you are going diving for the day, take it out of the freezer in the morning ready to heat up when you get home. If you don't have a huge saucepan, then halve the recipe and cook it for 6. This chilli is quite spicy, so add less paprika and chili powder for a milder one!
To make this chilli really rich and velvety, try grating 100% chocolate cacao into it.

Baked Fish in Crusted Sea Salt

Serves 2

Ingredients

1kg coarse sea salt
1 whole sea bream or sea bass gutted and cleaned
2 tbsp water
2 egg whites
A few bay leaves

Method

See method on p112 for how to prepare your fish.
In a bowl, mix the salt, egg white and water until you get a sludge-like consistency.
Put a layer of this salt mix on the bottom of a large roasting tin and pack well. Lay the fish on top with a few fresh or dried bay leaves.
Cover the whole fish in the rest of the salt mixture. Be generous and pack it well so it is solid and there are no gaps or holes.
Place it in a very hot oven around 220°C, gas mark 8, for about 20 minutes.
Now for the dramatic bit: take the fish out of the oven and douse it in vodka, tequila or Sambuca. Bring it to the table and set it alight quickly. Just wait for it to go out on its own. It will not stay lit for long.
Then, carefully, using a kitchen hammer or a dive weight, break the shell of the salt crust and push it aside carefully, making sure you don't damage the fish or push the salt into the cooked fish.
Use two large fillet knives to serve onto heated plates.
Setting the fish on fire is just for entertainment, but you have to try it. It's so much fun to watch your guests' faces and it definitely gives this dish the WOW factor. I first learned of this recipe when I was working in Malta in a restaurant called Tarragon. There, they made it with Lampuki. It was fabulous and probably the most popular dish on the menu.
This is a great way to cook fresh fish straight from the sea.

Top Tip

If you don't have a fillet knife and fork set, which most people don't, just use a cake slice it does the job just as well. Horseradish and crème fraiche sauce goes really well on the side. Mix 5 parts crème fraiche to 1 part horseradish with some fresh chopped parsley sprinkled on top and a drizzle of olive oil.

Sliders

Serves 4

Ingredients

500g beef mince
2 sausages
2 tsp Cajun sea spice mix
Salt and pepper
4 x slices of mature cheese (optional)
4 x burger buns of your choice

Method

In a bowl, use your hands to mix together the mince, skinned sausages, Cajun spice mix and salt and pepper. Make sure all the ingredients are well combined.
Form 4 patty shapes and refrigerate them for at least an hour or until you need them.
Place on a suitable baking tray and cook in the oven for 20 to 25 minutes until the juices run clear. Turn the sliders half way through cooking.
Cut your buns in half and lay the bottom half on a clean baking tray, place the burger on top and then the cheese (if you are using it). Then place the other half on top of that.
Put them in the oven for 5 minutes or so, until the cheese has melted and the bun is hot.
I alternate between brioche buns, seeded burger baps and sourdough rolls, when I can get them.
I serve them with my fresh, crunchy salad and homemade coleslaw.
We have been serving sliders since the very beginning, as everyone likes a burger, especially Al. It is believed that the term slider came from the Navy where greasy burgers were called sliders because they could slide down so easily. That's Al's story anyway. Of course my burgers are not at all greasy!

Top Tip

You can just grill these burgers or you can use a griddle pan. As I cook 12 at time I use the oven and that works really well.
Sometimes, if there is leftover bacon from breakfast, I put a slice into Al's slider. (Make these sliders the night before and they taste even better.)

Mackerel Straight From The Sea

Serves 1

Ingredients

Freshly caught mackerel, preferably still wriggling
1 tsp of Cajun Sea Spice (page 156)
30g melted butter
Freshly chopped parsley
Sea salt and black pepper

Method

Gut your mackerel, clean with fresh water and dry. Make an incision just behind the pectoral fin and run the blade of the knife horizontally next to the main central bone towards the tail of the fish to produce a fillet, turn the mackerel over and repeat.
Clean with fresh water and dry.
Melt the butter and brush over the fillets, sprinkle with Cajun Sea Spice, season with sea salt and pepper and grill immediately for 10-12 minutes. No need to turn them over as we only need to just cook them.
Sprinkle with freshly chopped parsley and a wedge of lemon or lime. This is food of the Weather Gods!
I serve these mackerel on fish and chip night as an alternative to breaded cod, along with chips from our deep fat fryer and crushed peas with rocket. It's a winner every time.
We keep a fishing rod on the top deck for keen divers, who are looking for something to do in between dives. When we have too many fish I just keep cooking them and make mackerel pate. Nothing gets wasted. Eventually I have to confiscate the fishing rod!

Top Tip

Something else I do, is cut the fillets into 5 or 6 bite-sized pieces, depending on the size of the fillet, and grill them as above. Then I stick a cocktail stick in each one and pass these nautical niceties around before dinner as an appetizer. They go fabulously with a beer or a gin & tonic.

Sea Bream Stuffed with Sausage Meat

Serves 1

Ingredients

1 sea bream gutted and scaled.
2 pieces of streaky bacon
1 lean sausage (Walls sausages work really well)
A few sprigs of thyme
1 tsp olive oil with 1 tsp melted butter
Wedge of lemon

Method

Scale your fish first in the bottom of the sink to keep the scales from flying everywhere.
Cut off the fins and back spines with kitchen scissors. Then, working from tail to head,
scrape off the scales using the back of a knife. Wash, dry and then gut by slitting the belly
from the head to the anal fin. Hoick out the guts with your fingers and discard. Snip out
anything left behind. Then, under running water, work the knife down the backbone to
scrape away any remaining blood.
Rinse thoroughly then dry thoroughly using a paper towel.
Open up the cavity and season well
Squeeze out the sausage from its skin and stuff it into the cavity.
Season it well and close the cavity up.
Wrap the two pieces of bacon around the fish to hold it in place and slip the thyme
underneath the bacon.
Brush the fish with a mixture of melted butter and olive oil and lightly season the fish all
over.
Bake in a pre-heated oven at 180°C, gas mark 4, for 30 to 40 minutes and cover it after 20
minutes to keep the moisture in.
Take the foil off 5 minutes before serving it with a wedge of lemon.
This is a fantastic dish and so easy to do. It looks really impressive wrapped in streaky
bacon with fresh thyme.

Top Tip

Crème fraiche and horseradish sauce works really well as an accompaniment to the dish,
along with a few chips and, of course, a squeeze of lime. I describe how to make the
crème fraiche and horseradish sauce in the Top Tip on page 106.

Diver-caught Surf and Turf Scallops

Serves 2

Ingredients

A goody bag of, say, a dozen scallops
Butter
Cajun Sea Spice (1 tsp per 12 large scallops)(See page 156)
3 bacon rashers cut lengthways
Sea salt and pepper
Freshly chopped parsley
2 wedges of lemon

Method

Clean your scallops. If you don't know how, ask a fellow diver.
Wrap six of them in bacon and use a cocktail stick to hold the bacon in place. Leave the other six unwrapped.
Put the butter onto a baking tray and melt it in the oven for a minute.
Take the tray out and scatter the scallops on it, then sprinkle them with the Cajun Sea Spice and season well.
Bake in a pre-heated oven at 180°C, gas mark 4, for about 15 minutes until the bacon looks crispy and the scallops are just cooked. You can always test one without the bacon when nobody is looking!
Serve sprinkled with freshly chopped parsley and a wedge of lemon or two. I usually serve these on Fish and Chip Night if we have caught some.
This recipe is just amazing and incredibly simple, especially if you have made my Cajun Sea Spice recipe in advance.
I remember I first saw scallops in their shells in 1990 at a hotel where I was working as a chef. We had fresh fish delivered every day, and on the hand-written invoice were the words "diver-caught scallops". I was so impressed. I was just learning to dive and hoped one day to catch my own.

Top Tip

Don't add too much Cajun Sea Spice or it will spoil the delicate taste of the scallops. Just a little sprinkle is enough to really enhance the taste of these little bites of deliciousness. The reason I only wrap half the scallops is because too much bacon can overpower the dish.

Spicy Pasta Scallops

Serves 2

Ingredients

A small goody bag of 10 scallops
½ tsp Cajun Sea spices
120g linguine, (or your choice of pasta)
60g chorizo sausage, chopped
Sea salt and pepper
½ red pepper thinly sliced
2 spring onions thinly sliced
1 small red onion thinly sliced
1 tbsp small capers
1 tbsp balsamic vinegar
Freshly chopped parsley
1 tbsp of sweet chili sauce
100ml of crème fraiche

Method

Clean your scallops ready for cooking, rub them in Cajun Sea Spice and set them aside.
Put the pasta on to boil for about 10 minutes. Then drain and set aside.
While your pasta is boiling, heat up a heavy frying pan, add the chorizo and cook for a few minutes until it is soft and you have plenty of fat in the pan.
Add the onions, red pepper and scallops and fry gently for about 5 to 7 minutes, turning occasionally.
Add the crème fraiche, capers, balsamic vinegar and sweet chilli sauce and stir gently.
Once it is just bubbling, it is ready to serve. Add the cooked pasta and toss all the ingredients together.
Sprinkle with parsley and serve immediately with a green salad.
This recipe is similar to a dish served by a restaurant we know in Malta. I loved it and have tried to replicate it. It is perfect for feeding two hungry Salutay crew on a Friday night after we have cleaned the boat from top to bottom.

Top Tip

Add a little white wine to loosen up the sauce if it seems a bit thick, and don't forget to have a slug yourself just to check it's OK.

Fresh Catch in a Pouch

Serves 2

Ingredients

2 x 130-150g of fish of your choice skinned and bone free
2 leaves of cavolo nero cabbage with stem removed (or kale or spinach)
6 cherry tomatoes on the vine
2 x 15g slices of Ginger and Lime Butter (See page 156)
1 tbsp small capers
Olive oil
Sea salt and pepper

Method

Cut two pieces of Bacofoil (2 in 1 Parchment and Foil: Bake, Shape, Create) into 30 x 30 cm squares. Lay the squares flat on a work surface and pour a splash of olive oil in the middle of each square.
Then scatter the cabbage about and place the fish on top with the tomatoes around the edge of the fish.
Cut two 15g slices of Ginger and Lime Butter (see page 156) and place one on top of each fish. Scatter the sliced red pepper and capers over and season. Pull all four corners of the Bacofoil together to form a pouch.
Place them on a baking tray and cover with another lighter baking tray on top. (So you don't have to worry if your pouch is open at the top).
Bake them in a pre-heated oven for 20 minutes at 180°c, gas mark 4.
Serve immediately. I serve them with chips because we have a deep fat fryer on board. They taste even better at sea after a great dive.
This is a really great dish and so simple, especially if you have made some Ginger and Lime Butter in advance. If you haven't, use a mix of 15g butter, ½ tsp of grated lime zest, ¼ tsp of grated ginger and a good grind of black pepper instead and divide between the two fish.

Top Tip

If you didn't manage to catch any fish that day then salmon from the freezer works well too. It will defrost in no time.
The pouches are perfect for cooking at sea: I have no worries about them leaking when the boat moves. Of course it has to be calm for the deep fat fryer to be turned on.

Fish Chowder

Serves 2 (large portions)

Ingredients

1 tbsp olive oil
1 x 400g packet of sustainable fish pie mix
8 sustainable prawns (any size: the larger the better)
2 spring onions chopped
1 onion roughly chopped
120g soft goats cheese with chives (plain goats cheese is fine too)
100ml milk
100ml chicken stock
1 lime
A few chives for the garnish
Sea salt and pepper

Method

Heat the olive oil, add the onions and sauté gently until soft.
Add the goat's cheese, milk and stock.
Bring just to the boil.
Add the prawns and simmer for 5 minutes, then add the fish and cook gently for about 10 minutes.
Season to taste and garnish with freshly chopped chives, a wedge of lime and a fish-shaped crouton, if you are feeling creative.

Top Tip

The dish is so quick and easy to do, so have the ingredients in the fridge ready to cook as soon as you get home from your dive. It goes fabulously with crusty bread.

Ratatouille

Serves 4

Ingredients

1 red onion,
1 large white onion
4 garlic cloves
1 aubergine
3 courgettes
2 red peppers
1 yellow pepper
6 ripe tomatoes
½ a bunch of fresh basil
2 tbsp of olive oil
3 sprigs of fresh thyme
1 400g tin of quality plum tomatoes
1 tbsp balsamic vinegar
½ a lemon

Method

First prepare your vegetables. Peel and cut the onions into wedges, then peel and finely slice the garlic. Trim the aubergine and courgettes, deseed the peppers and chop them into chunks.

Heat up a couple of glugs of olive oil in a large saucepan over a medium heat, add the aubergine, courgettes and peppers and fry for about 5 minutes until softened, but not cooked through.

Spoon the cooked vegetables into a large bowl and set it aside.

Add the onion, garlic, thyme leaves and chopped basil stalks with some extra olive oil and fry for 10 to 15 minutes or until soft and golden, being careful not to burn the garlic.

Return the set aside vegetables to the pan and stir in the quartered fresh tomatoes along with the tinned, the balsamic vinegar and a good grind of sea salt and black pepper.

Mix well, cover the pan with the lid and simmer on a low heat for about 30 minutes until reduced, sticky and sweet.

Garnish with basil leaves and lemon zest.

All you need now is the Pork Loin Steak Stack (see page 102) to go with it and a few roast spuds!

Top Tip

This dish is better made in advance, I make it in the afternoon straight after lunch, so that it has time to sit and mature. It also means I've got time to go for a quick second dive.

Quinoa Stuffed Pepper

Serves 1

Ingredients

1 large red or yellow pepper
Olive oil
1 small cup of quinoa
2 small cups of boiling vegetable stock
A knob of butter
3 spring onions, finely chopped
¼ of a deseeded red chili finely sliced
10 cashew nuts
Sea salt and pepper
4 slices of hard goat's cheese or grilled halloumi cheese

Method

Cut the pepper in half lengthways keeping the stalk the best you can and deseed it.
Rub the inside with olive oil and season it.
Place it on a small baking tray and cover with silver foil. Bake in a pre-heated oven at 180°C, gas mark 4 for 15 minutes, then set aside.
Put the quinoa in a saucepan with the vegetable stock and bring to the boil, then cover with a lid and simmer for 15 to 20 minutes, until the liquid has been absorbed.
Fluff up with a fork and set aside.
In a separate pan melt the butter and fry the spring onions and chili until soft.
Add the cashew nuts and season.
Add the cooked quinoa and mix together to form a stuffing.
Spoon the stuffing into the pepper and pack well, leaving no gaps.
Bake in a pre-heated oven at 180°C, gas mark 4 for 20 minutes then take it out, put the cheese on top, crack some black pepper over and pop it back in the oven for 5 minutes until just melted.
Serve with fresh parsley and a wedge of lime.
This is a great vegetarian meal. Quinoa is a complete protein and a good alternative to couscous.

Top Tip

You can cook the pepper in advance, let it cool and stuff it later. I serve this meal with leftover ratatouille, as they go extremely well together. This is a great vegan meal too if you use vegan cheese and oil instead of butter.

Mackerel Pâté

Ingredients

400g freshly cooked flaked mackerel in Cajun Sea Spice (fine bones removed)
200g light cream cheese
1 tsp good quality horseradish
Juice of one lemon
Sea salt & cracked black pepper

Method

This is a great way to use up leftover cooked mackerel that you cooked in the Cajun Sea
Spice (see page 110).
Flake the mackerel into a bowl.
Take half the mackerel and put it in a food processor with the cream cheese, lemon juice
and horseradish.
Whiz it all together and season to taste.
Scrape it out into the bowl to join the remainder of the flaked mackerel and mix
everything together carefully.
Serve it in ramekins or small jam jars and sprinkle with fresh parsley, more cracked pepper
and a tiny drop of olive oil on top.
Serve with toasted bread fish. Cut the fish shapes out of sliced bread and toast them
under the grill.
This pâté freezes very well.

Top Tip

Had enough of mackerel for now? Then freeze the remaining cooked mackerel it into
portion sizes and use it another day. You will be so glad you did.

Chicken and Ham Pie

Serves 6 (large portions) 24cm round pie dish needed

Ingredients

Filling
1 tbsp of olive oil and 30g butter
1 white onion chopped roughly and 4 spring onions sliced
100g black kale, sliced into small pieces
1 large carrot peeled and chopped into small pieces
30g plain flour
200ml chicken stock (1 stock cube) and 60ml crème fraiche
340g cooked chicken (dark and brown meat) torn apart
110g cooked ham chopped into small chunks

Pastry
340g plain flour, 115g baking margarine and 60g lard
100ml cold water and a pinch of salt

Method

Heat up the olive oil and butter in a deep pan and fry the onion, kale and carrots until soft.
Add the flour and stir it in well being careful not to let it stick to the bottom of the pan.
Add the chicken stock slowly, stirring continuously until there are no lumps, then add crème fraiche and stir in.
Add the torn chicken and ham and plenty of seasoning.
Mix well and set this aside while you make the pastry.
Place the margarine, lard, flour and salt into a food processor and crumb. Cut the lard into pieces first so that it is easier to work with.
While the machine is still turning slowly, add the water and let a lump form.
Turn it out onto a floured surface and divide into two pieces, one slightly bigger than the other.
Roll the larger piece into a circle slightly bigger than your pie dish and place it carefully inside the dish so that it rolls over the edge.
Trim around the edges using a sharp knife.
Tip your pie mix into the lined pie dish and use a palate knife to smooth it flat.
Brush the edges of the pastry with some milk ready for the top.
Roll out other piece of pastry to make the pie lid, using more flour if necessary.
Place this carefully on top of the dish and trim around the edges.
Crimp the edges of the pastry with your fingers to make a seal. Work with one hand on the inside of the edge, and one hand on the outside. Use the index finger of your inside hand to push the dough between the thumb and index finger of your outside hand to form U or V shape flutes.
Continue to do this all around the pie plate, spacing your flutes about an inch apart.
Make a deep hole in the centre of the pie and brush with milk all over.
Decorate the top with leaf shapes using the left over pastry.
Brush the leaves with milk and cook in the centre of the oven at 180C, gas mark 4, for 45 to 60 minutes until golden brown.

Originally these pies were made using turkey instead of chicken, because Al's mum reared turkeys for 28 years up until 1999 and as you can imagine there was plenty of turkey available. In fact, when I started, the menu was mostly turkey! Turkey curry, turkey pie, turkey casserole: the bronze turkeys were the best.

Top Tip

Instead of making one big pie, you can make 6 individual pies with this recipe, using mini pie dishes. One pie makes the perfect lunch for a day's boat diving.

Pollock, Chorizo, Butterbean, Spinach & Goat's Cheese Skillet

Serves 4

Ingredients

4 x 140g - ish pollock fillets (whatever you catch), bones and skin removed
½ a Spanish cooking chorizo, cut into strips
4 spring onions chopped
200ml chicken stock
1 large bag of baby spinach washed
100g soft goat's cheese
400g canned butterbeans, rinsed and drained
Sea salt and pepper

Method

Place the fish on an oven tray, greased with butter and olive and season. Cook at 180°C, gas mark 4, for roughly 20 minutes.

In a skillet or whatever frying pan you have, fry the chorizo until it is soft, add the spring onions and cook gently. Add the goat's cheese, stock and butterbeans and cook for 5 to 10 minutes to heat through. Season to taste.

Just before serving, add the spinach and slowly wilt. Place a lid on top to keep it warm.

To serve, take the lid off the skillet and place the fillets of fish on top.

All you need to go with this mind-blowing dish, apart from a good bottle of white wine, is some wonderful French bread, but if you are stuck at sea then dig some sourdough out of the freezer. It is just as good.

Top Tip

Always use a sustainable fish. Pollock works so well with this dish because the sauce is so flavourful that it brings the pollock to a whole new level. This is a dish that you can cook when you get home after a dive in no time at all.

131

"It's so much easier cooking in the galley than at home, especially when the view from the window changes constantly. I'm so lucky!"

Chicken Contata & Chicken Stuffed with Haggis

Chicken Contata

Serves 4

Ingredients

4 large chicken breast fillets
4 bacon rashers
280ml chicken stock

Stuffing
240g mushrooms, finely chopped
1 garlic clove crushed and 2 spring onions, finely chopped
60g fresh wholemeal breadcrumbs
30g butter
1tbsp olive oil
Sea salt and pepper

Sauce
60g butter and 60g flour
140ml milk
2 tbsp crème fraiche
100g grated mature cheddar cheese
20g flaked almonds

Method

Slit the chicken breasts to form a pocket. Set them aside.
Heat the olive oil and butter in a heavy based deep frying pan, then add the mushrooms, garlic and onion and sauté for 3 to 4 minutes.
Add breadcrumbs, salt and pepper and mix thoroughly. When it is cool, divide into 4 portions and stuff the chicken breasts. Wrap a bacon rasher around each one, securing it with a cocktail stick.
Place in a casserole dish. Pour the stock over and cover tightly with a sheet of foil. Cook it for 35 to 40 minutes at 180°C, gas mark 4. Ten minutes before adding the sauce, remove the foil to make the bacon crispy.
For the sauce: melt the butter and add the flour to make a roux. Gradually add the milk and casserole stock. Bring to the boil and simmer for 1 minute. Add the crème fraiche. Season to taste. Pour over the chicken, sprinkle with cheese and almonds. Return to oven for 5 to 10 minutes. Serve with champ and green veg.
This recipe came from Iris, Al's Mum. It's been replaced in our menu with the chicken and haggis recipe, but I still make it sometimes for a change or when I can't source haggis. It was a real favourite of Terry Goldie's. He would only come on a trip if I promised to make it.

Top Tip

You can freeze the whole dish and re-heat it slowly in the oven once it has thoroughly defrosted.

Chicken Stuffed with Haggis, Wrapped in Bacon

Served with a whisky & wholegrain mustard sauce

Serves 2

Ingredients

2 chicken cutlets or 2 chicken fillets
2 streaky bacon rashers
1 thick slice of good quality haggis cut in half (in a half moon shape)

Sauce
2 tsp of whole grain mustard
½ tsp of Dijon mustard
75ml crème fraiche
Stock made from cooked chicken and haggis
Sea salt and pepper
A good splash of single malt whisky

Method

Use either chicken fillets or chicken cutlets, which are chicken fillets with the wing bone left in.
Butterfly the chicken breast to make a pocket, push the haggis in and mould it with your hand, then wrap the bacon tightly around each chicken breast and place in a deep oven tray.
Season them with a good grind of black pepper and sea salt. Cook in the oven for 30 minutes at 190°C, gas mark 5.
Remove from the oven, scoop up the juices using a small ladle and pour them over the chicken, then cover with silver foil and cook for a further 15 to 20 minutes.
Put all the ingredients for the sauce in a saucepan, apart from the chicken stock, and heat gently. Just before serving, drain the chicken juices into the sauce and pour it all over the chicken.
Serve with champ, carrots and kale. Champ is an Irish dish made by combining mashed potatoes and chopped spring onions with butter, milk and seasoning.
I first brought this recipe in when we ran our 4-days trips from Oban diving the Sound of Mull because it was so apt. We were in Scotland and haggis was readily available. It proved so popular that I continue to make it now. We have it on a Sunday evening as the first dinner of the trip, normally in Cherbourg or sometimes at anchor in the Baie de Seine.

Top Tip

A good single malt is the making of this sauce. I usually raid Al's whisky collection (but I also keep a cheap bottle in the galley so he doesn't suspect).

Laughs at the RNLI charity fish supper on board

Desserts from the Galley

Apricot, Peach, Mango & Ginger Crumble

Serves 12

Ingredients

Crumble topping
300g self-raising flour or gluten-free flour
150g butter or dairy-free spread
120g Demerara sugar
2 tsp ground ginger

2 x 250g tin of mangoes (drained and sliced)
20 fresh apricots quartered and stones removed
3 fresh peaches or a 410g tin of peaches (drained)
Drizzle of maple syrup or honey
30g chopped pecan nuts

Method

Using an electric mixer, mix the crumble ingredients to a crumb-like consistency and set in the fridge until needed.
Place the sliced fruit in a large, deep ovenproof dish and mix up thoroughly. Drizzle over the syrup or honey, then tip the crumble mix over the fruit and spread it out evenly.
Bake it in the oven at 180°C, gas mark 4, for 30 to 40 minutes, until the crumble is oozing from underneath and golden on top.
Sprinkle the pecan nuts over the top and serve with custard, of course, or indulge yourself with a dollop of clotted cream on the side. That's what I normally do while I'm washing up in the galley. (Shush, don't tell the divers!)

Top Tip

You can cook this crumble in advance and warm it up later. It will be even juicier. It's easy to make this crumble gluten-free and dairy-free. Just replace the flour and butter with gluten-free and dairy-free alternatives.

Ships Trifle

Serves 12

Ingredients

240g Italian sponge fingers
1 x 290g tin of mixed berries in light syrup (drained weight-110g)
2 tbsp good quality strawberry jam
200g frozen mixed berries
500g readymade good quality vanilla custard
150ml whipping cream
150ml Mascarpone cheese
1 punnet of fresh strawberries
30g fresh mint

Method

Using half the sponge fingers, make a layer in a deep glass bowl.
Then put the jam over the top followed by another layer of fingers.
Drain the juice from the mixed berries into a jug, and pour over the sponge fingers to make them moist.
Using a spoon, pour the tinned berries over the top along with the frozen berries.
Whip the custard, cream and mascarpone cheese together and spread evenly over the sponge and fruit.
To serve, scatter chopped or sliced strawberries over and top lavishly with slithers of fresh mint leaves.
This is a delicious combination. I love seeing the divers' eyes light up when I bring this pudding out.
Every week when I bring out a pudding like this made for 10, and deliver it to one of our two 5-person tables, someone will say "Great, we've got ours. So, what's the other table having?" Every week without fail! Ha-ha!

Top Tip

I use home made strawberry jam made by my friend Ann. She makes enough to take us through a whole season (see page 157). You can make individual trifles if you prefer, which is what I do sometimes when I have people with different dietary requirements on board. Or sometimes when I just fancy a change. Pop a viola flower on top if you are at home and they are in season as they are edible and look beautiful.

Banoffee Pie

Serves 10-12 (depending on the server's generosity)

Ingredients

270g ginger nut biscuits (crumbed)
90g butter
Two 397g tins of Carnation caramel (condensed toffee)
2 ripe bananas
300ml double cream
30g dark chocolate flakes
6 strawberries cut in half lengthways

Method

Crumb the ginger nuts using a food processor. If you don't have one, put your biscuits in a strong plastic bag with a tea towel on top, to stop the bag from splitting, then use a dive weight to smash them. This works just fine.

Melt the butter in a pan, add the ginger nut crumbs and mix until the crumbs are evenly coated in the butter.

Tip the biscuit mixture into a serving dish making an 8-inch circle. Press it down carefully to make a base.

Chill for several hours.

Spread the condensed toffee evenly over the base.

Whip up the cream until it is just whipped. It's easy to over-whip double cream so be careful.

Slice the bananas and scatter them over the toffee layer.

Spread the cream evenly over the bananas and decorate with strawberries.

Use a potato peeler to make lovely dark chocolate flakes and sprinkle them all over.

Top Tip

You can now buy Carnation Caramel (condensed toffee) in most supermarkets, so there is no longer any need to boil your own. Years ago, I would have to boil around 50 tins in advance of each season.

Key Lime Pie

Serves 12

Ingredients

The Base
270g ginger nut biscuits
90g butter

The Filling
1 x 380ml tin of condensed milk
450 ml double cream
The zest and juice of 5 limes (no chance of getting scurvy on the Salutay)
30 dark chocolate

Method

Line a 10-inch spring bottom cheesecake tin with greaseproof paper (or you can just use a flan dish).
Crumb the biscuits using a food processor. If you don't have one use a strong plastic bag covered with a tea towel and use a dive weight to smash them. I had to do this once when the generator was down and I couldn't find my rolling pin.
Melt the butter in a pan and add the ginger nut crumbs, then mix until the crumbs are evenly coated with butter.
Tip the biscuit mix into the tin, pressing it into the base.
Chill for about an hour.
Pour the condensed milk, double cream, lime juice and zest into a mixing bowl. Mix thoroughly until you have a thick consistency. Don't worry if it doesn't seem thick enough. It **WILL** set in the fridge.
Tip it over the base and leave it overnight.
To serve - release the spring bottom of the tin and carefully place it onto a serving dish. If you have used a flan dish then it's ready for the next stage.
Melt the dark chocolate in a small bowl in the microwave. (Yes, we have a microwave on board).
Using a teaspoon, drizzle the melted chocolate in lines across the pie.
Set it in the fridge until you are ready to serve.
A microwave was fitted on board in 1988 and, for 28 years, it was used mainly for heating up plates, as I have a thing about food being served on hot plates. But one day during a trip, it just stopped working. We replaced it immediately on the next turnaround day.

Top Tip

For best results, make this dessert the day before. It sets perfectly and the flavour of the limes becomes really zesty and tangy. This is so delicious after my curry halfway across the Channel.

Al dressed up for the D-Day parade, Port en Bessin Normandy

Extras from the Galley

Skippers Overnight Porridge

Serves 1

Ingredients

1 banana
150g natural yogurt
10g chia seeds
40g porridge
1 kiwi fruit chopped
A few blueberries and raspberries
30g Omega seed mix ground
A drizzle of honey if desired

Method

Using a hand blender, blend the yogurt with the banana in a large jam jar.
Add the porridge and chia seeds and mix well.
Leave the mix to rest for 5 minutes, stirring occasionally.
Peel and chop the kiwi fruit and place it on top along with the blueberries and raspberries
and seed mix. Put the lid on it and leave it in the fridge overnight. In the morning, you're
going to be so glad you made this the day before!
Grab it, sling in your dive bag and enjoy it on the way out to the dive site. Your dive
buddies will be jealous and you won't be wanting to eat anything until lunchtime.
Don't forget to bring a spoon with you.
This is a fantastic breakfast to have before a day of diving either from a hard boat or rib. Al
has his in the early hours when we do our overnight steams across the channel.

Top tip

You could just top it with some granola instead of seeds. Basically you can adapt the
toppings to your liking.

Cajun Sea Spice

Ingredients

1 tsp red pepper flakes
1 tsp coriander
1 tsp onion granules
1 tsp garlic powder
1 tsp paprika
1 tsp cumin
½ tsp oregano
¼ tsp black cracked pepper
¼ tsp sea salt

Method

Using a coffee grinder, grind up all the ingredients together.
Pour them into a jam jar.
Use a clean paintbrush to get all the spices out of the grinder.

Top tip

I use this spice mix for lots of my recipes. It's a great mix to have on board and it's so versatile. I use a tablespoon of each instead of a teaspoon when I want to make a bigger batch.

Naina and Raj's Garam Masala

Ingredients (all dry)

200g coriander
100g cumin
100g cloves
50g cinnamon
50g cardamom seeds
4 whole nutmegs (broken up)
5g fennel feeds
6 pieces of star anise
100g black peppercorns
50g ginger
25g bay leaves

Method

Place all the dry ingredients on a baking tray and bake at 100°C on a low heat for one hour. When they are cool, grind them all together in a coffee grinder and pour them into a glass jar with a lid.
Garam Masala is made with whole spices that have been roasted and then ground.
Naina and Raj Mistry are keen divers and have dived with us on the Salutay in the Channel Islands. This is their recipe for Garam Masala that they took from an original recipe of Naina's Mother and Raj's Aunt and have now made their own.
Beware -it's a little hotter than most Garam Masala recipes and a little goes a long way.
Use this to make our Cross Channel Curry (see page 100).

Top tip

You can break a whole nutmeg by placing it on a cloth and bashing it with a meat mallet, a rolling pin or even a dive weight!

Ginger and Lime Butter

Ingredients

2cms fresh root ginger peeled and grated
Zest of 1 un-waxed lime
Juice of ½ a lime
100g butter
Cracked black pepper - a good grind

Method

Place the ginger, lime zest and juice, butter and pepper in a small food processor and blend them until the butter is smooth.
Place the mixture in the centre of a piece of greaseproof paper or cling film, roll it up and keep it chilled until you need it.

Top tips

If you can't buy an un-waxed lime then just put the lime in a colander and pour water over it from a recently boiled kettle. Or rinse the lime under a hot running tap.
The easiest way to peel ginger is to use a teaspoon. Scrape the edge of the spoon against the ginger to peel off the skin.
You can freeze Ginger and Lime Butter. Just cut it into slices beforehand and use it as needed.
It goes great with scallops. Melt some butter in a pan and sauté your scallops to perfection.

Crushed peas for fish and chips

Makes 12 portions

Ingredients

1kg bag of petits pois (frozen peas)
100g butter
Sea salt and pepper
1 bag of rocket

Method

Bring the peas to the boil for just a few minutes and drain immediately. Add the butter, season and blitz them quickly to a crushed consistency using a hand blender.
Add the rocket and, just before serving, mix through very gently using a spatula. Crushed peas with rocket go so well on Fish and Chip Night and make a great alternative to your usual mushy peas.
I buy sustainable breaded cod, but serve freshly caught mackerel when we have managed to catch some.

Top tip

To make this dish for 4 to 6 people, use half a bag of frozen peas and less butter. It's amazing how a large bag of peas goes down to nothing when they are blitzed and a great way of eating more peas! Or just make the recipe for 12 and freeze what you don't use.

Tartar sauce

Serves 12

Ingredients

60g capers drained
A 345g jar of mayonnaise of your choice

Method

Using a small food processor, blitz the capers for less than a minute so they still look bitty. You do not want a smooth paste. Scrape them into a bowl with the mayonnaise and mix together using a spatula. Pour into a serving dish and keep in the fridge until you are ready to serve. This tartar sauce may sound rather simple, but it is just De-lic-ious! And it is fab with most fish.

Top tip

Quarter this recipe to make it for 2-3 people. Any leftovers will keep well in a jam jar for 2 weeks and you will never buy ready-made tartar sauce again!

Ann's Chilli and Apple Jelly

Ingredients (for 4 x 250ml jars)

1000ml of 100% apple juice -no sugar or calcium added.
900g preserving sugar
½ tsp butter
2 tsp mild chilli flakes

Method

Pour the juice into a large pot along with the butter.
Heat over a low heat, slowly stirring in the sugar for about 4 minutes.
Add the chilli flakes and bring the mixture to a full rolling boil, stirring/skimming regularly until it reaches setting point at 105°C (usually after about 20 to 25 minutes). A good jam thermometer is very useful.

Ann's Strawberry Jam

Ingredients (for 4 x 250ml jars)

1kg ripe tasty strawberries
750g jam sugar
the juice of one lemon
½ tsp of butter

Method

Wash, dry and hull the strawberries, then crush them lightly with a potato masher.
Put them in a large pot along with the butter and lemon juice.
Stir over a low heat until the strawberries soften.
When they have softened, slowly stir in the jam sugar.
When all the sugar is dissolved, bring the mixture to a full rolling boil stirring regularly until the mixture reaches setting point at 105°C (usually after about 20 minutes). A good jam thermometer is very useful.

(**For both recipes.**) Test for setting by putting a teaspoonful on a cold saucer and turning it upside down. If it does not drip, it is set.
Transfer to hot sterile jars and seal them immediately.
I usually sterilise the jars with boiling water and pop them in the oven at the lowest setting for about 10 minutes.
They should keep for up to a year if properly sealed.
These are my favourite preserves in the world! My friend Ann very kindly makes me enough for a whole season and the divers love them at breakfast! The strawberry jam also goes in my Ships Trifle (see page 142). Thank you Ann!

Coleslaw

Serves 12

Ingredients

1 pointed white cabbage
3 carrots
1 red onion
500g mayonnaise
1 tbsp freshly-chopped parsley
Sprinkling of paprika

Method

This coleslaw is extremely easy to make and is so much nicer than bought coleslaw.
Using a sharp knife, slice the cabbage in half lengthways and remove the core.
Then cut it into quarters lengthways, thinly slice and place into a large bowl.
Slice the onion in half and cut fine slithers, then peel and grate the carrots and add to the bowl. Add the mayonnaise and mix thoroughly using a metal spoon.
Sprinkle with paprika and chopped parsley.
Now you are ready to make sliders (see page 108).

Sprouting at Sea

I have been sprouting seeds at sea for as long as I can remember. It's a great way to have a constant flow of fresh organic vegetables packed with vitamins ready to garnish your meals with and they look absolutely fabulous too. I used to try and grow herbs but they just don't seem to like the sea air so much.

I keep my little sprouter in the galley. It's in constant use throughout the season and it seems to love it there. I keep it well wedged in now after it hit the galley floor and cracked after a big wave hit the side of the boat. I thought the non-slip mat would be enough, but it wasn't.

There are many seeds to choose from for sprouting, but these are my favourites.

Alfalfa Sprouts

Alfalfa sprouts come from a germinated alfalfa seeds and are a great, nutritious addition to many meals. When the seed germinates, it creates a shoot, which is then harvested before the plant matures fully.

Despite their tiny size, these sprouts contain a ton of vitamins, minerals and nutrients that can provide plenty of benefits for your body. They will be ready in six to eight days. You can buy them in your local health food shop

Red Clover Sprouts

These sprouts grow from organically produced seeds. Red Clover sprouts look like alfalfa sprouts, have a mild, sweet flavour and are a brighter green. They are easy to grow and an excellent source of vital nutrients. They will be ready to eat in 3 to 5 days. Again, you can buy these in your local health food shop.

Little Radish Sprouts

These pack a strong, spicy punch and are ideal for accompanying salad ingredients with less flavour. This sprouted radish seed contains reasonable amounts of vitamin A, iron, and calcium and loads of vitamin C. That should help keep the scurvy away! Harvest them once the seed has produced a significant length of stem or after 3 to 5 days. Once again, get them from your local health food shop.

Mung Bean Sprouts

Mung beans are great for sprouting. They are crisp and add a slightly nutty taste to any meal. You will find them in most supermarkets. You can grow bean sprouts in as little as 2 to 3 days. They are also great for stirfrys.

All you have to do is rinse your seeds and spread them onto each tray.

Pour around half a litre of water into the top tier. The water should slowly but steadily drain down. The surplus water tray at the base of the germinator should be emptied after each watering. Check that all the excess water has drained down from all three layers.

Top Tip

If you do one tray of seeds then leave a few days before you do the next tray and then the same again with the third tray, you wont have all three trays ready to eat at the same time. Then just rinse each tray twice a day under cold running water, drain well. The sprouts seem to flourish in the sea air. I think they love it!

Acknowledgements

Al and I would like express our appreciation to: Leigh Bishop, Mike Clark, Claire Goodwin, Jos Greenhalgh, Rohan Holt, Bruce Humby, Steve Jones, Innes McCartney and Richard Ward for some of the incredible photographs in the diving section. Without these photographs this book would not have been possible. Special thanks to Rohan Holt and Steve Jones.

We would really like to thank Simon Pridmore and Sofie Hostyn for making this book become a reality.

We would also like to thank Innes McCartney for organising the Operation Deadlight expeditions: it was great to be a part of that, with all that historical maritime history on our doorstep.

A huge thank you to Peter Wright – Al's Dad (Chief Engineer) for being on hand when we had engine room issues. He was always just a telephone call away.

I would also like to thank Al for his patience when we were photographing the 40 dishes. It wasn't always easy having me as the food stylist!

And to all those divers who have nagged us to write a book! Well here it is! We've finally done it!

And to Jan and Dave who owned and operated the Harry Slater liveaboard, Jan was an amazing cook and has always inspired me. They are sadly no longer with us. Miss you both dearly.

I never thought I would still be cooking for divers after nearly 20 years and still loving it! I get a different view every minute of every day from my galley window. And I am so lucky to have been able to do such phenomenal diving all around the UK and Ireland. Thanks Al.

Freda Wright

August 2018

Photo Credits

All the images in this book are by Al and Freda Wright and self-explanatory, except: -

P13 HMS Audacious, Malin Head by Steve Jones
P14 RMS Justicia, Malin Head by Steve Jones
P17 Empire Heritage by Steve Jones
P23 Freda & Al on the SS Laurentic bow by Jos Greenhalgh
P23 Laurentic 6 inch gun by Jos Greenhalgh
P27 U2511 Elektroboot by Innes McCartney
P29 Tory Island -Tornadrallagh by Rohan Holt
P32 Al and Gary Sharp by Danny Burton
P33 The Lusitania's steam whistle discovered and photographed by Leigh Bishop in the late 90s: the heart and sound the one of the most elegant ships that ever sailed the ocean
P34 Basking shark by Rohan Holt
P37 Rathlin North cliffs, Farganlack Point by Claire Goodwin
P38 Rathlin's first arch at 25 to 30m: diver Stephanie Bennett, by Claire Goodwin National Museums, Northern Ireland
P39 Guillemot off Rathlin Wall by Rohan Holt
P40 Freda feeding congers on the wreck of the SS Templemore, Ballycastle by Mike Clark
P43 The Saw Cut at St Kilda, by Al
P44 The stunning Scarbhstac arch at St Kilda by Rohan Holt
P45 Flying minke whale by Rohan Holt
P45 Soay lambs at St Kilda by Rohan Holt
P46 Seal at the Sound of Mull by Steve Jones
P47 The Harry Slater: with fond memories of Jan & Dave
P55 Mike Morris by Freda
P58 Lovely divers in new tee shirts, Ron Bruijn, Mike van Nikkelen Kuijper, Tjerk Bouwman, Hans Paapen, Onno Kok, Al, Joeri Vinkx, Camiel Brants
P59 The Empire Broadsword by Steve Jones
P62 Sark, Channel Islands by Richard Ward

£1 from the sale of this book will be donated to Greenpeace UK's ocean plastics campaign. You can find out more at www.greenpeace.org.uk
Thank you for buying this book

GREENPEACE

Seal photo by Steve Jones

Made in the USA
Columbia, SC
03 September 2018